ENDORSEMENTS

This insightful and provocative book will assist those who are serious about fulfilling prophetic destiny to develop their inner man as the essential prerequisite to successful achievement of their external goals.

—Bishop Harold Calvin Ray
Senior pastor of Redemptive Life Fellowship

In a world desperate for answers, Tim Timberlake's book, *Abandon*, offers real help and spiritual guidance to the challenges we all face. Tim's insights are lifted right out of our everyday lives yet deeply rooted in the truth of Scripture.

With his finger on the pulse of today's culture, Tim is a leader for today. His honesty and transparency connect with people, and his is a voice that we've been waiting to hear.

In *Abandon*, readers will relate to the stories Tim shares and find themselves thinking long and hard about the principles Tim outlines to help us discover a better way to live.

—Roland Hairston, II
Publisher, *Gospel Today*

Tim Timberlake is an authentic Christian man on a mission to change this world. He has proven through the years his willingness to do whatever is necessary to live out God's future for him. His engaging, enlightening, and life-changing book will help you to do the same. It's time to let go and let God bring you into the amazing future that He has for you!

—ANDRE BUTLER
Pastor of Word of Faith International Christian Center
Author of *God's Future for You*

Tim Timberlake is a voice for the digital generation. His life is about impacting people so that they can live a relevant life outside the box. His book, *Abandon,* forces you to think about your personal life story and how to transform your future without sacrificing your faith.

—HAJJ FLEMINGS
@HajjFlemings
Founder of Brand Camp University

The new book, *Abandon,* by Tim Timberlake is exactly what the Kingdom needs. His offering is replete with concise nuggets of wisdom to navigate life and reach the destination assigned for the life of the believer. *Abandon* encourages the reader to lay aside the weights that hinder forward momentum. A must-read.

—BISHOP JASON NELSON
The Tabernacle at GBT
Stellar Award-winning singer/songwriter

Tim has an incredible knack and God-given ability to help anyone who has the desire to gain crystal clarity of God's desired plan and purpose for their life. *Abandon* is a strident call to leave the old things behind, ditch the doubt, and take the exhilarating step into the path that God has for your life.

—SCOTT WILLIAMS
@ScottWilliams, Church growth/leadership consultant
and strategist at NxtLevel Solutions
Author of *Church Diversity* and *Go Big*

Choices, challenges, and changes. Tim Timberlake's *Abandon* is a spiritual handbook for anyone struggling to fully give their life to Christ. By taking an in-depth look at the life of Jacob (one of my favorite Bible characters), this book shows how to see God's faithfulness as the greatest reminder, in any situation, of the radical love and grace He's already given us.

—STEVEN FURTICK
Lead Pastor, Elevation Church and *New York Times*
best-selling author of *Crash the Chatterbox, Greater,* and
Sun Stand Still."

Many of us are on a monotonous quest at this juncture of life. It's a quest to search for something that's strong enough to satisfy the yearnings that surpass our mind but stem from the core of our soul. Despite the effort exerted, the yearnings have yet to be quenched. What a lot of us don't realize is, the things that we are walking toward are the very things we must turn away from in order to find satisfaction. In this compelling body of work, *Abandon*, Pastor Tim affords you the opportunity to experience a truth that eloquently teaches: satisfaction is an achievable end result but not independent of the process of abandonment. I am fully confident that the words penned on these pages will prove to be more than a book, but rather, a catalyst for abiding, long-lasting change.

—REVEREND DARRELL PATRICK

Tim Timberlake has written an insightful and inspiring book that will help you in your everyday life to win the battle between what you want and what God truly desires for your life. The first thing I did was reach for my phone so I could share some of these practical nuggets of wisdom.

—JUSTICE COLEMAN
Freedom Church, Los Angeles, California

ABANDON

ABANDON

Laying Aside Your Plan for God's Purpose

TIM TIMBERLAKE

DESTINY IMAGE® PUBLISHERS, INC.

P.O. Box 310, Shippensburg, PA 17257-0310

"Promoting Inspired Lives."

This book and all other Destiny Image and Destiny Image Fiction books are available at Christian bookstores and distributors worldwide.

Cover design by Eileen Rockwell

For more information on foreign distributors, call 717-532-3040.

Reach us on the Internet: www.destinyimage.com.

ISBN 13 TP: 978-0-7684-0671-9

ISBN 13 eBook: 978-0-7684-0672-6

For Worldwide Distribution, Printed in the U.S.A.

1 2 3 4 5 6 7 8 / 19 18 17 16 15

DEDICATION

To my father, Bishop Mack Timberlake—I am who I am today because of what you instilled in me. You loved me, you challenged me, and you changed my life forever by being the epitome of a great father. When I look in the mirror, I see you. When I speak on the various platforms God has granted me, I hear you. And although I miss you greatly, I am comforted by the memories that remain. As long as I live, you live.

To my anchor, my mom, Pastor Brenda Timberlake. You have been there for me every step of the way. Your strength strengthens me. Your courage pushes me to be more courageous. Your love for me is unending. Thank you for seeing in me what others couldn't. I love you!

ACKNOWLEDGMENTS

There is no way possible I can list everybody who has imparted something in my life that has made me the man I am today. So the first line, I will leave blank—if you don't find your name in this section, go ahead and fill it in. The other names listed below are the precious people who were directly instrumental in bringing this project to life.

Nica, Darrell, Chris, Tim, Quis, Maj, TT, Micah (Da Fam)—I love you, and I'm honored that we do life together as siblings.

Ms. J (Aunt Joynee)—Thank you for always believing in me! You'll find Uncle Mark's wisdom sprinkled all throughout this book.

Bishop Keith Butler, Pastor Deborah Butler (Mom and Pop)—Your continual investment into my life continues to blow my mind, and I am forever grateful.

Jason Yarborough (Yarby) a.k.a. Brother from Another—There would be no book without you believing in me! Love you with all my heart!

Bishop Jason Nelson (the Singing Prophet)—Thank you for speaking and singing life into me!

Mike Worley (Mikey Mike)—You made this possible!

Wade Olinger (The Connector)—Thanks for believing in me!

Bryan Scott (B. Skizzle)—Thanks for seeing creativity when I can't!

Jamie Calloway-Hanauer—Thank you for putting the pieces together!

Bishop Harold and Pastor Brenda Ray (Unk and Auntie)—Thanks for believing in me! I love you!

To all of my uncles and aunties, I love you all!

Dre, Tif, Mimi, Krissy, Joel, Steph, Larry, Lisa, Kev, Nita, Efo, Beazzle, Odie, Bri, B, Arod, Herm, Darrell Patrick, Darrell Edmunds, J, Hajj, Jeff, Kierre, Roland, Levi, Monica, Micah, Chey, Alex, Marcus, Nisa, Chris Ray, Johnny, Chrissy, Reggie. We talked about this many nights; thank God it's finally here!

To the church I serve, Christian Faith Center! You all are the best church this side of Heaven! The best is yet to come!

CONTENTS

FOREWORD

The book you are holding in your hands is not one to be taken lightly. As you go through this book you will laugh, you will think, and most of all you will grow through Tim's revelation on this message of Abandonment. It will give you, the reader—the inspiration you need to strengthen your relationship with Jesus regardless of where you are in your faith.

If we all were to be brutally honest, we know what it is like to feel like everything is going in the opposite direction of what we may have planned or thought. In times like that, the ability to give the control over to God makes all the difference. It gives us Godly direction; and it sets us on the charted course God has laid out for us. *Abandon* will cause you to look up for your help, and look inward for your change, it reminds us that if we are willing to leave the old behind in search of the life God desires for us to live, He will give us a life far better than the one we Abandoned.

Tim's genuine challenge to Lay Aside Our Own Plan for God's Purpose is timely, bold, and emphatic. Pick up this book with an earnest and expectant heart, lay aside your own ambitions, and discover God's dream for your life, and begin to live a life of purpose.

—MIKE FOSTER

INTRODUCTION

Don't let the title of this book fool you.

When we hear the word *abandon*, our first thought is usually a negative connotation—such as giving up, settling, forgoing responsibility, or leaving something behind.

In this book, I am asking you to throw out the negative images that come from the word *abandon*, and instead realize that the act of abandonment can actually bring you closer to God and closer to becoming the disciple of Christ you long to be.

This book is going to require you to take some action, roll up your sleeves, and put it all on the line. It's going to ask you to leave behind—*abandon*—your selfish, unhealthy, self-gratifying ways. That may sound like a task for someone else. After all, you're a good person, right? You don't have selfish and unhealthy ways, right? Before you put this book down and walk away, thinking about someone else who may need to read it, may I suggest that we all have things we need to abandon to bring us closer to God? Sure, for some people these are the things society has deemed big, dark, and "bad"—drugs, sex addiction, illegal behavior. But take a moment to consider the "smaller" things—coveting your friend's relationship with his or her spouse, envy toward that person who does less than you do but gets paid more, unwarranted anger taken out on your kids, the little white lies you tell to get what you want when you want it. Do any of these sound familiar?

For most of us, they do. And each item listed (and more), small as they may seem, works its way between you and the very God who made and loves you and has a perfect plan and will for your life. To close that distance between you and God you must take each of those items—the large and the small—and abandon them for a life of righteousness and obedience to Christ.

As uncomfortable and scary as that may sound, there is no need to be afraid. In fact, you should take great joy in knowing that our Holy Redeemer has a plan made especially for you that no one else can live out: "'For I know the plans I have for you,' declares the Lord, 'plans to prosper you and not to harm you, plans to give you hope and a future'" (Jeremiah 29:11 NIV). Even when times are tough and the water is rough, there's a future with your name on it. When I think about this—*God has a will and plan for me!*—I become filled with joy. In fact, I can't tell you how big I smile every time I realize there's a great big God in Heaven who is thinking about me and all the great things

He intends for my life. Do you feel this joy on a daily basis? What about even a couple of times a week? If not, why?

Perhaps it's because you have let your connection to things of this world and your desire to do things "your" way get the best of you. Perhaps it's because temptations beckon you and you don't quite know how to say "no" to their call or protect yourself from their enticement. You hear the sweet siren song, and it lures you in. I know how that feels because it's something everyone—even me—has experienced at one point or another. And it isn't fun. It feels like being tossed at sea, no compass to point us in the right direction and no indication of when—or if—we'll ever see dry land, sturdy and solid under our feet, again.

In fact, in the book of Acts, Paul *is* being tossed at sea, and all indications are that he and his fellow shipmates won't live long enough to make it ashore. Their ship is caught in a raging fourteen-day storm, during which they are sure they will die (see Acts 27:20). On day three of this storm, Paul shared with the other men that he had been visited by an angel and that there was no need for them to fear for themselves:

And now I exhort you to be of good cheer: for there shall be no loss of any man's life among you, but of the ship. For there stood by me this night the angel of God, whose I am, and whom I serve, saying, Fear not, Paul; thou must be brought before Caesar: and, lo, God hath given thee all them that sail with thee. Wherefore, sirs, be of good cheer: for I believe God, that it shall be even as it was told me (*Acts 27:22-25*).

Can you imagine the response Paul got? His shipmates probably wanted to toss him overboard. Paul, however, remained firm in his conviction. God had told Paul that not a single man aboard the ship would be killed, and it was with this comfort in mind that Paul assured his shipmates that not a single one of them would be lost, but that only the ship would be destroyed.

While his fellow shipmates likely found Paul crazy or, at best, annoying in his cheer and certainty, Paul was absolutely right about how things would end. More importantly, Paul not only believed God would keep him safe during the storm once it was over, but his faith in God was a comfort to him in the *midst* of the storm, as well as a witness to the others aboard about God's power. What Paul was saying was, "Don't abandon ship! Instead, abandon your fear. Abandon your reliance on what you think you know is to come. Abandon your desire to do it your way. Instead, trust God to get you through." Paul wanted us to feel the impact of God's glorious message on our own lives: Not one of His followers can be lost; only the ship will be destroyed.

We may not be stuck on a ship in the middle of the ocean, sailing with a bunch of prisoners during a fourteen-day storm, but we have our own storms to weather. If you're like most people, you don't even know where to begin to find the courage Paul had in the middle of great turbulence. You don't know how to abandon your ways to follow the will of God; you don't know how to feel the deep goodness of being lost in the right direction. That's what we are going to address in this book—the *whys* and *hows* of abandoning self to God, going willingly in whatever direction God points you. To do this, we will look to the Bible and follow the life of Jacob, son of Isaac and grandson of Abraham. Jacob, a man who had to learn the hard way how to believe in and lean on God's will for his life, and who eventually became known as Israel, Father of the Nations.

THE STORY OF JACOB

For those unfamiliar with the story of Jacob and his family, contained within the book of Genesis, I'll give you a quick synopsis of it here. It is imperative that we visit this story in order to understand what Jacob had to endure to become the man God intended for him to become. Like all of us, he was a person who had to make incredible sacrifices and *abandon* his will in order to follow the will of God. Jacob's story and relationship with God will be revisited frequently as we move through each chapter of this book.

###

Finally pregnant after years of trying, Rebekah and Isaac were thrilled. But Rebekah suffered a terrible pregnancy, feeling every possible ill effect there was. Finally, desperate as the baby within tossed and turned mercilessly, she cried out to God. Rebekah was shocked to hear His reply: she would bear twins—two sons, who even now were wrestling within her. The sons would become two nations, and the older would serve the younger. Rebekah could not understand what this meant—two nations? How? But Rebekah was a woman of faith, and she trusted God's Word.

Rebekah did indeed give birth to twin boys—Jacob and Esau. Esau was born only seconds before Jacob, and Jacob held fast to Esau's ankle as the two struggled to be born. Little did Isaac and Rebekah know that this simple act was a foreshadowing of how Jacob and Esau would live their lives: Esau being first, and Jacob struggling to rise to the top. Even as he grew, Esau could feel the imprint of Jacob's fierce baby-grip on his ankle—a phantom sensation, the mark of a broken relationship, just as Jacob felt the need to pull himself higher.

It is unknown and hard to determine why, but Rebekah favored Jacob over Esau and treated them each differently. She babied Jacob, keeping him close to her side at home, where she taught him the ways of homemaking.

Esau, on the other hand, was his father's favorite. Unlike Isaac who was weak, old, and passive, Esau was big and strong, a hunter and outdoorsmen. But for all his strength, he also carried a strong odor and was very hairy. He never felt quite comfortable in his own skin, and he despised being the oldest child—bearer of the birthright. Birthright is an enormous privilege, one for which Esau should have been thankful. But he wasn't. He was instead focused on hunting and securing game and being free of responsibility.

Esau loved the outdoors, loved the feel of the dirt beneath his feet, the wind blowing strong through his hair. He went out for days, only returning when he had to. It was hard to be home, where every day it was made clear that his mother preferred Jacob, his twin. Although Esau was his father's favorite, Isaac had rendered himself almost irrelevant within the household, letting Rebekah lead and manage in most manners.

Jacob and Esau Make a Deal (Genesis 25:19-34)

After one of his days-long excursions, Esau returned, famished, to the family home, where he found Jacob in the kitchen, standing over a pot of stew. Their mother had taught Jacob how to cook; she had not taken the time to teach Esau.

"Brother," said Esau. "I am famished! Give me stew, and fast!" Esau was faint with hunger.

Still stirring the stew, his back to Esau, Jacob responded, "I will give you stew in exchange for the birthright."

Esau was taken aback. Stew for birthright? What was this about? But really, Esau didn't care. He was starving, and he hated the responsibility of the birthright anyway.

"Sure, brother. Now give me stew!"

Although it appears Esau gave up his birthright for stew, in reality Esau had given up his birthright far earlier when he had put everything but family first and taken for granted that he was the eldest son, favored, and destined to oversee the family's affairs.

What was done was done—fair and square Jacob and Esau had made a deal, and Esau no longer had the birthright. Jacob had finally pulled Esau down and moved above him.

The Deceiver (Genesis 27:1-41)

Some time later, as Isaac grew weak and close to death, he told Esau to go out and bring him fresh game to eat. Then Isaac would pass to him the blessing of the firstborn, the sacred privilege that would make Esau the heir and successor to his father, the head of the family.

Rebekah, knowing Isaac's intent, called Jacob, her favorite, to her. "Jacob, you must go to your father. You must have him give you the blessing of the firstborn!" In her influential role as mother and understood head of household, in this way Jacob learned deceitfulness at Rebekah's feet.

In the moment, taken aback as he was, Jacob was unsure how to respond. "But he'll know it's me!" he argued.

"No, here. Wear this—it will make your arms seem as hairy as your brother's," and she put a coat on him. "Now take this game to your father—it is his favorite!"

It all happened quickly, and Jacob did as he was told. He went cautiously to his father.

"Here is your food."

His father reached out and grabbed Jacob's arm and felt the coat's fur under his hands.

"Funny," said Isaac. "You sound like Jacob, but feel like Esau. Is it really you, Esau?"

Jacob lied to his father, making assurances that he was indeed Esau, and Isaac prayed the blessing of the firstborn over Jacob:

> *May God give you heaven's dew and earth's richness—an abundance of grain and new wine. May nations serve you and peoples bow down to you. Be lord over your brothers, and may the sons of your mother bow down to you. May those who curse you be cursed and those who bless you be blessed* (Genesis 27:28-29 NIV).

Mere moments later, Esau burst through the door, eager to serve his father the game he had caught. He approached Isaac with the food. When Esau spoke, Isaac trembled violently and his voice shook as he realized he had been tricked by Jacob. He told Esau what had happened and Esau feel to his knees, pleading with his father: "Bless *me*—me also, oh Father!"

But Isaac had given his only blessing away; none was left.

Isaac said to Esau, "Indeed, I have made Jacob your master, and all his brethren I have given to him as servants; with grain and wine I have sustained him. What shall I do now for you, my son?"

And Esau lifted up his voice and wept.

Then Isaac said to him: "Behold, your dwelling shall be of the fatness of the earth and of the dew of heaven from above. By your sword you shall live and you shall serve your brother; and it shall come to pass, when you become restless, that you shall break his yoke from your neck."

And so the Lord's word from so long ago had come true: the younger would rule the older.

"I will kill him!" Esau stormed from the house, too angry to contain his violent feelings. Rebekah, upon hearing Esau's word, called Jacob to her once again, this time to tell him to flee to her brother, Laban. "Stay a few days," she implored him. "Esau will calm down, then I will send for your return." Rebekah additionally hoped that while Jacob was with Laban, he would take an appropriate wife for his own.

Rebekah shared her thoughts with Isaac. "Husband, if Jacob should take a wife from the wrong clan, what will become of me? My life will be worth nothing." Understanding his wife's deep worry, Isaac commanded Jacob, "Take a wife from the daughters of Laban." So Jacob left to begin his long journey to Laban's home.

Jacob Meets God (Genesis 27:41–28:22)

On his way, Jacob grew weary. He lay down to sleep and, while sleeping, dreamed. He dreamed that a ladder from Heaven reached down to earth and that angels were walking upon it. The Lord God stood above the ladder and said:

"I am the Lord God of Abraham your father and the God of Isaac; the land on which you lie I will give to you and your descendants. Also your descendants shall be as the dust of the earth; you shall spread abroad to the west and the east, to the north and the south; and in you and in your seed all the families of the earth shall be blessed. Behold, I am with you and will keep you wherever you go, and will bring you back to this land; for I will not leave you until I have done what I have spoken to you."

Then Jacob awoke from his sleep and said, "Surely the Lord is in this place, and I did not know it. If God will be with me, and keep me in this way that I am going, and give me bread to eat and clothing to put on so that I come back to my father's house in peace, then the Lord shall be my God."

Jacob continued on his journey, finally coming upon a flock of sheep and a group of men. As Jacob stood and talked to the men, he saw a beautiful woman approach. It was Rachel, daughter of Laban. They embraced in greeting, and Rachel then ran to her father to announce the good news of Jacob's arrival.

Jacob Deceived (Genesis 29–31)

Jacob stayed in Laban's home for a month and worked for him. In return, Laban attempted to pay Jacob fair wages. Jacob, however, was not interested in money. Instead, he asked for the hand of Laban's youngest daughter, the beautiful Rachel.

"I will serve you for seven years," he said, "if you will give me Rachel in marriage."

Laban agreed. Jacob served Laban for seven years, but the years seemed to fly by to Jacob because he knew his reward at the end would be great—the love of his life would become his bride.

When the seven years had ended, Jacob said to Laban, "Give me my wife, for my days are fulfilled, that I may go in to her." But it came to pass in the evening that Laban took Leah, his oldest daughter, and brought her to Jacob, and in the morning Jacob beheld that he had been with Leah. Furious, Jacob approached Laban, "What is this you have done to me? Was it not for Rachel that I served you? Why then have you deceived me?"

Laban scoffed at Jacob's anger and said, "It must not be done so in our country, to give the younger before the oldest. Fulfill a week, and we will give you Rachel for serving with me still another seven years."

Jacob, deeply in love with Rachel, agreed, and after he had served one week, Jacob also went in to Rachel, and he loved Rachel more than Leah. And he served with Laban still another seven years.

The deceiver had been deceived, but Rachel had become his.

Years passed, and after many struggles and pleading with God, both Leah and Rachel bore children to

Jacob. Jacob, wanting his parents to meet his wives and children, asked his leave of Laban.

"Send me away, that I may go to my own place and to my country. Give me my wives and my children for whom I have served you, and let me go; for you know my service which I have done for you."

Laban replied, "Please stay, if I have found favor in your eyes, for I have learned by experience that the Lord has blessed me for your sake." Then he said, "Name me your wages, and I will give it."

But Jacob only wanted one thing—to return to his home. He thought for a moment about how he might get what he wanted. He was struck with a plan, and he responded to Laban, "You know how I have served you and how your livestock has been with me. For what you had before I came was little, and it has increased to a great amount; the Lord has blessed you since my coming. And now, when shall I also provide for my own house?"

So Laban said, "What shall I give you?"

And Jacob said, "You shall not give me anything. If you will do this thing for me, I will again feed and keep your flocks: Let me pass through all your flock today and remove all the speckled and spotted sheep, and all the brown ones among the lambs, and the spotted and speckled among the goats; and these shall be my wages. So my righteousness will answer for me in time to come, when the subject of my wages comes before you—every one that is not speckled and spotted among the goats and brown among the lambs will be considered stolen, if it is with me."

And Laban said, "Oh, that it were according to your word!" So he removed that day the male goats that were speckled and spotted, all the female goats that were speckled and spotted, every one that had some white in it, and all the brown ones among the lambs, and gave them into the hand of his sons. Then he put three days' journey between himself and Jacob, and Jacob fed the rest of Laban's flocks.

Jacob, blessed with deep intelligence, separated the sheep such that the speckled and spotted would conceive only with each other, and thus produce many speckled and spotted lambs. He put his own flocks by themselves and did not put them with Laban's flock.

Over time, Jacob mated the feeble sheep with other feeble sheep, and likewise stronger sheep with one another. So the feebler were Laban's and the stronger Jacob's. And this is how Jacob became rich and had large flocks, female and male servants, and camels and donkeys.

Laban became poor and Jacob became rich, and Laban was angry at what he perceived as Jacob's deceit. Jacob felt Laban's anger and was worried. Jacob heard the Lord speak to him. The Lord said, "Jacob, lift up now your eyes and see that all the male goats which are mating are striped, speckled, and mottled; for I have seen all that Laban has been doing to you. I am the God of Bethel, where you anointed a pillar, where you made a vow to Me; now arise, leave this land, and return to the land of your birth and I will be with you."

Jacob gathered his wife, children, and belongings, and began the trek back home.

Along the way, it occurred to Jacob that, once home, he would have to face Esau. Worried, he devised a plan. He sent messengers ahead to Esau to tell him that he wanted things to be right between them. The messengers returned shortly with their own report: "Esau is on his way to meet you! He has 400 men with him!"

Jacob thought fast. If Esau were coming to attack him, how could Jacob fight back? Again, Jacob devised a plan, born of his fear of Esau's retaliation.

"Let us divide into two groups. At least then if he attacks one group, the other will be left."

Nonetheless, Jacob was concerned. "God," Jacob prayed, "You promised me safe passage! What is this about Esau coming after me with 400 men? I pray You keep Your word and deliver me from his hand!"

Jacob then sent messengers out again, this time with presents for Esau, so that Esau might not remain angry at Jacob. In so doing, he acknowledged the wrong he had done to Esau.

A Fight for Blessing (Genesis 32–33)

Jacob then set out on his own. He was alone and without the safety of protection or the comforts of his wives and children. He was scared, alone, and exhausted. Overcome, he sank to the bank of the Jabbok River, but before he could settle into an uneasy sleep, a man approached him. The man began wrestling with Jacob, and they wrestled until daybreak.

"I will not let you go until you bless me!" Jacob responded, fiercely pinning the man down along the banks.

So the man said to him, in order to bless him, "What is your name?"

"Jacob."

And the man said, "Your name shall no longer be called Jacob, but Israel—father of nations—for you have struggled with God and with men, and have prevailed."

Then Jacob asked, saying, "Tell me your name, I pray."

The man responded, "Why is it that you ask about my name?" And in fact, the man would not answer Jacob, and did not profess his name. But the man did bless him there.

So Jacob called the name of the place Peniel: "For I have seen God face to face, and my life is preserved." Just as he crossed over Peniel, the sun rose on him, and he limped on his hip, a changed man forever, destined for greatness. Jacob had wrestled God and prevailed, but he would forever bear the scars of their encounter.

Fear, Hope, and Blessings Received (Genesis 34–47)

Even though Jacob had been blessed with a visit from God, that did not change Esau's all-too-fast approach. As Esau and his men grew close, Jacob fell to the ground in respect. To his surprise, Esau ran to him, embraced him, and the two brothers wept as they rejoiced at their reunion. After a time, Jacob and Esau parted ways, and Jacob established his home in Canaan according to the word of God.

Jacob's children grew, and the family encountered many heartaches. The actions of his children brought embarrassment and hardship onto Jacob, and Jacob was displeased. To escape the hardship that his sons had brought upon him, Jacob and his family resettled in Bethel, where Jacob dedicated himself, his family, servants, and land to God. At that time, God came once again to Jacob, renewing his covenant and blessing with Jacob and his descendants:

> *Your name is Jacob, but you will no longer be called Jacob; your name will be Israel. ...I am God Almighty; be fruitful and increase in number. A nation and a community of nations will come from you, and kings will be among your descendants. The land I gave to Abraham and Isaac I also give to you, and I will give this land to your descendants after you* (Genesis 35:10-12 NIV).

After receiving this blessing from God, Israel returned to the land of his father, Isaac, who soon passed away, but not before he and Israel reconciled.

###

PHASE ONE

THE CHOICE

Our culture values independence.

We hear a lot about being self-made and people doing whatever it takes in order to achieve what society considers "success." Guys who live at home with their mom and dad for too long are looked down on, and being financially dependent on someone else is considered a sign of weakness. With all our society's focus on independence, it's easy to get the message that we better do this life thing alone, *our* way, or else we're lesser, weak, immature, or a complete and utter disappointment. These are, of course, standards made by man. As such, they fail to consider that independence from God is not a success, but rather a complete and total failure. Without daily reliance on God, we will surely flounder and fail, whether we still live in our parents' basement or whether we struck out on our own at the first chance we got. True success comes from giving our whole selves over to God to do with what He will. Believe in what God told you to do and success will follow.

While every person feels and experiences things differently than others do, there are several common problems that keep us from reaching this level of self-abandon in our walk with Christ. In this section we will explore those common problems and discuss how to avoid or, better yet, to overcome them. The first step is figuring out where our weak spots are—what are we holding on to that would be better let go? Haven't we all, at one point or another, hoped that perhaps God could just turn a blind eye "this one time," and that He wouldn't notice a certain situation? What barriers have we put up that we hope God won't notice? For many of us, it's having a case of the "If Onlys." The *If Onlys* cause us to want everything other than what we have and keep us looking to everything but God for fulfillment.

True success comes from giving our whole selves over to God to do with what He will. Believe in what God told you to do and success will follow.

#ABANDON

The *If Onlys* often go hand in hand with a case of "How Can I Fix This?" which is when we try to force our will and desires into being without any attempt at discerning God's plan for us. When our *If Onlys* don't happen, we create what we think to be the best scenario, which isn't God's best, often leaving us with a bit of a mess to clean up, and the overwhelming question of "How Can I Fix This?"

Even after we've torn these barriers down, we're often still left wondering *how* to live a life fulfilled through Christ. There's not an "If This Then That" solution, so you can stop trying to create the right situation for God to reveal Himself through some perfect storm. The answer, however, is easy. It's the application that's hard: *It is only through willingness and obedience that we will reach the righteousness we desire.*

> Disobedience in any area produces
> curses, and curses cause us to fail.
> #ABANDON

It will, without a doubt, be hard to reach the level of righteousness God desires for us to walk in if we have areas of disobedience in our lives. Disobedience in any area produces curses, and curses cause us to fail. On the flip side of that, when we adhere to the things God instructs us to do, it produces blessings. And the blessings of God empower us to prosper.

When you abandon all you are to Him, He will take you and mold you into the person He desires you to be. Don't worry about how "broken" or "damaged" you think you or the situation you are going through are; God can heal your heart and soul and make you whole again. When you really grasp this truth and start believing this, it will lead you to the abundance that both you and God desire for your life. Hesitation and disobedience to God's Word will get you nowhere; obedience, belief, and faith are what will see you through. Trust me when I tell you there are going to be plenty of times when you have to hold on to God's Word past the point of your comfort level. Sometimes you might wonder, "Where is God? Why isn't He in this moment? Why isn't my life going right?" It may sound cliché, but the truth is, even when it doesn't seem or feel like it, He's working it out for your good. This doesn't mean you pray and the next morning your life will make a complete 180 (although that's possible!). Instead, you and I must learn the hard work of waiting patiently for God's timing, being obedient to His Word, and watching His plan for our lives unfold. Of course, waiting patiently for God's timing can be hard work.

> Don't worry about how "broken" or
> "damaged" you think you or the situation
> you are going through are; God can heal your
> heart and soul, and make you whole again.
>
> #ABANDON

Chapter One

DON'T DO IT YOURSELF (DDIY)

Success isn't measured by how much we have gained or acquired. It's measured by our obedience to what God desires.

We are all uniquely made. We look different, talk different, have different backgrounds, and come from different walks of life. In fact, you can be certain that there are no two people on this entire planet who are identical in every way.

But for all the uniqueness we possess and the special identities we've been given, we all have at least one commonality: *we all have things in our lives that we need to abandon.* These are what hold us back from the righteous life we desire and the fulfillment God intends for us. Until we identify and abandon these holdups, we will live in discontent and disharmony, always wondering why life just doesn't quite seem right.

I've seen the enemy gain access to people's emotions (and from there take it further and further, until life seems like a hopeless cause) time and time again because they rush through life, off kilter, without making time to get straightened out, strengthened, and renewed in the presence of the Lord. They push aside the need to be silent, to be still, to rest, and to wait. As a result, their perception of things around them gets twisted and thrown out of balance. Doing too much too fast has worn them down, causing them to lose their focus and ability to see things the way they really are, and making them hold too tightly to things that are best released.

This problem isn't unique to our society or to today's culture. We know that from the beginning of time humans have done these same things. In fact, we see this reflected as early as Genesis, where we read the story of a dysfunctional family of four—Mom (Rebekah), Dad (Isaac), and two boys (Jacob and Esau) who, despite being twins, could not have been more different. For all their differences, Jacob and Esau both had things they needed to abandon. Jacob, younger than Esau yet prophesied to rule over him, was anxious to take what he could as soon as humanly possible to achieve his higher status. Esau, spoiled by his father and handed the family birthright simply by virtue of being the older twin, took for granted all that he'd been given.

Esau needed to abandon his spoiled ways, and Jacob needed to abandon his desire for immediate gratification and status. Both of these character's flaws come to a head in the book of Genesis, where Esau easily disregards his privileges and Jacob barters and deceives his way into the privileged role.

FLAW #1: IF ONLY...

Jacob, Esau, Isaac, and Rebekah would fit right in on one of today's reality shows. Spoiled Esau, petulant and deceitful Jacob, scheming Rebekah, and checked-out, irrelevant Isaac. Frankly, there is probably some of them in all of us, especially Jacob.

Jacob's greatest character flaw—independently pursuing desires, no matter the cost—is unfortunately common. We have this tendency to hold tight to something we place great value on, such that we would lie, cheat, steal, and use trickery to get it, just as Jacob did. In those moments, we would do *anything* rather than abandon our heart's desire for something out of reach, or to be someone—anyone!—other than who we are. Instead of waiting patiently to see the fruits of God's will, we push forward with selfish calculation to achieve instant gratification.

I know you've done this before, just as I have, because I know that we're all just humans with selfish desires of the flesh and the false belief that things would "only be better if...." If we had more money, more freedom, more cars, less responsibility, fewer kids, or a more attractive spouse. If we could just have someone else's life, or someone else's things, all would be better.

> Instead of waiting patiently to see the fruits of God's will, we push forward with selfish calculation to achieve instant gratification.
>
> #ABANDON

This attitude fails to consider the God-given truth that He will give us just what we need, just when we need it.

FLAW #2: IGNORING GOD'S TIMELINE

It's hard to look around and see friends and family getting the things you want. Maybe all your friends are already married with kids, or they got to go to college and you didn't. Maybe your best buddy just got a promotion and is making the salary you've always dreamed of making while you're still sending out resumes and knocking on doors. Whatever the case may be for your life, there's little doubt that it's tough not to feel let down when it seems everyone is doing better than you are.

In those times when you feel like life just hasn't caught up to where you want to be, take a step back and honestly assess where you are versus where you want to be. Ask yourself *why* you want to be somewhere else, and examine whether you're actually taking the right steps to get you there.

If you honestly feel you're doing the things that will eventually take you to the place God desires you to be, then don't panic and just keep doing what you're doing. You're already in a good place, filling yourself with God's Word, presence, and community; all you have to do is wait patiently. The things God has planted for you have simply not yet fully come to be. And that's okay. Maybe you're in the single-and-eating-instant-noodles-in-your-apartment season right now. Maybe you're in the overwhelming-and-sleepless-night season of raising a young family. Wherever you are, try to sit back and enjoy it while also taking, or continuing to take, the steps necessary to get you where you want to be next.

If you've reached the point in life that has you thinking it might be time to take the birthright and run—perhaps you hate your job, or your spouse has become more roommate than soul mate and you spend most nights wondering how things went so terribly wrong—that's when the time is right to stop listing the *If Onlys* and start understanding that God has made many difficult sacrifices to give you your unique identity. Trust Him to give you a life you that does not need escaping from, and start living the life that God has already given you, because the greatest manmade schemes and ideas *won't help you become a better you.* They will only create bigger, more harmful barriers between you, God, and living a life fulfilled.

FLAW #3: HOW CAN I FIX THIS?

Early on in the story, we saw Jacob take matters into his own hands. He asks himself, "How can I get what *I* want? Be who *I* want to be? How can I fix this situation to *my* liking?"

You see, Jacob looked to *himself* for the fix. In fact, the name "Jacob" represents independence from God. Sure, our society values independence, but independence from God is never a good idea. Instead, we must do exactly the opposite: *we must give our entire selves freely to God.*

I know that sounds scary. It's hard to let go of something we're used to holding so tightly. But abandoning your life to God isn't about losing control. It's about placing the control back where it belongs—in the hands of the very one who created us, who knew us before we were in our mother's womb, who has a purpose and a plan for us, and who deeply desires us to move from just existing to living a life fulfilled (see Jeremiah 1:5; 29:11; John 15:16). It's time to stop worrying about the *how* and put your trust in the *who.*

FLAW #4: GIVE ME VERSUS MAKE ME

Using a worldly and self-focused perspective, it's no wonder Jacob tried such crazy things to take what Esau had—the Bible describes Esau as a real "man's man" and the favorite son of their father. Jacob, on the other hand, was "a plain man who lived in tents" and made soup, a mama's boy (see Genesis 25:27). Not very impressive sounding, is it?

But for all his manly strength, Esau lacked Jacob's intelligence. Jacob had no trouble figuring this out, nor did he have any qualms about using his superior intellect—a misuse of his gift from God—to get what he wanted.

Much like Jacob, when we don't like who we are or what we do, we begin to compare our lives to the lives of others. When we make these comparisons, almost without fail we find that other people seem to have better lives than us, and we try to capture what they have and transform ourselves into something we're not. The problem with this is that *we can never be who God intended us to be if we're struggling with all our might to be like someone else.* I can hear your argument already—"But, Tim! I'm just trying to be so much better than who I am. I'm trying to *improve* myself. Wouldn't God want that?"

Improvement is one thing; fighting God's will is another.

It is, of course, easy to confuse the two. We live in a world that loves to make comparisons. In fact, our economy thrives off comparisons. Think of some of the most popular shows on television and what comes to mind? Shows about who looks the best, how to dress like your favorite celebrity, or how to be thinner/smarter/richer by doing what someone else has done. We can't go pick up a gallon of milk at the grocery store without encountering countless magazine headlines screaming out all the ways we should be different than we are so we can live and look more like the sleek, sexy, famous actor or model on the cover.

Back in Jacob's day, the comparison would have been to those around him with more prestige and power. And Jacob, of course, was a twin—and as a twin, there was likely no end to the comparisons made between him and Esau. Esau was their father's favorite, and the one to hold the birthright. So Jacob looked at Esau—strong and the favorite of their father—then back at himself—weak and the favorite of their mother (see Genesis 25:28). According to the standards of his time, Jacob perceived himself as "less than."

We can certainly imagine just what that felt like to Jacob. We're made to feel this way nearly every day by society.

When I was a young boy, Christmas was my favorite time of year. I was especially excited about Christmas when I had been very good. In the days leading up to Christmas, my parents would tell my siblings and me to make a wish list of all the things we wanted, and if we were really good we would get those things—at least one of them, anyway. I would excitedly make my list and be on my best behavior waiting for Christmas morning to come around. We would wake up early and head for the tree, where we would tear open our presents. I remember that I was always so happy with what I had gotten. I felt like I had hit the Christmas present jackpot. But as the morning calmed down and I began to look around to see what my brothers and sisters had gotten as their presents, I felt a little less happy. Their presents seemed better, somehow, than mine. Cooler, more exciting, more fun. Or maybe I counted mine and only got to ten, but when I counted my brother's or sister's presents, I counted twelve. Perceiving that I was lacking something, I went from elated to deflated, and felt the hurt of being less than. When I compared what I had to what they had, in my mind I came out the loser.

I imagine Jacob felt just like this, but even more so, because he wasn't just counting his siblings' presents—he was counting the very worth he had in his parents' eyes. He would have felt like the lowest of the low, never good enough for his father, spending his time hanging out in the kitchen with his mom, cooking the meat Esau had hunted down and brought home to feed the family.

Unfortunately, Jacob didn't realize that God would never anoint him to be anyone other than who he already was, and so he continued to dwell on his self-defined "problem" of being "less than" Esau, instead of giving thanks to God for being the very person God created him to be.

God would never anoint him to be anyone
other than who he already was.

#ABANDON

Instead of comparing and wanting to be someone else, can we agree to try a different approach? Can we agree to abandon the manmade mentality of who we "should" be, and cooperate with God to be His version of who we already are? You are a rare, one-of-a-kind, valuable, and precious child of God. It's time you started believing that.

But how?

JACOB REDEEMED: HOW CAN I BE WHO GOD WANTS ME TO BE?

Being who God wants you to be is a two-step process. You must be *willing* to follow Him, and then you must actually follow through by being *obedient* to what He is directing you to do.

Be Willing

Taking the first step by deciding to be a follower of Christ is just the beginning of your long journey hand-in-hand with God. There will be times when you feel God's presence more than at others, and it will be up to you to readjust your course when you are feeling "off." This willingness to readjust comes from your love for God and from believing He knows what's best for you. Being willing is actually the easy part; it means, among other things, that you pray when you can and read the Bible when you can. You even go to church if there isn't a big game on or you aren't too tired from a late Saturday night out.

But willingness is empty if it isn't coupled with obedience. Being willing without being obedient is a bit like saying you're sorry but then doing the same thing over and over again—willingness is easy, obedience is hard. And while the "sorry" is important for placing yourself in a position of humility in front of another, it's value really comes in the future action (or non-action, depending on what we're talking about).

It's the same with willingness and obedience. There's value in humbling yourself before God, saying boldly, "Mold me, God, into what You want me to be. Use me, God, for Your good work according to Your will." But the *true* value comes after that. The true value comes in each and every act of obedience to God's answer to your willing supplication. It cannot be, "Mold me, God, except for asking me to give up my powerful job. I need this powerful job so I can feel good about myself and make money for my family. God, I would be willing, but I'm just scared I won't be able to pay my bills if I follow the path I hear You telling me to take." There's no obedience in this action, just confirmation that you will do things your way because you either aren't really sure God will be there to see you through— such as to make sure you can pay your bills—or you simply don't like the direction He's pointing you.

It's funny how clearly we can see this in other people's lives. When we see this happening to our friends or family, it's easy to give them the advice that they need to "let go and let God." And when we say it, we believe it. We know that's the right way to live and the right thing to do. But when it comes to applying that truth to our own lives...well, that's an entirely different story. Isn't it amazing how easily we can see other people's shortcomings, mistakes, and wrong turns, but how difficult it is to see our own?

In the beginning of his story, Jacob seemed to have the "willing" part down pretty well. When blessed with a vision from God (Jacob's dream), Jacob praised God and vowed to worship Him…should God choose to keep Jacob in the way he wanted to be kept. But for all his willingness, Jacob failed to reach the level of "obedience" he needed. This is in fact why the renaming was necessar—unless and until Jacob gave his all in obedience to God, God could not do His work in Jacob.

I would guess that for a lot of you reading this book, this probably describes you. You've got the "willing" part down; it's the "obedient" part that trips you up most of the time.

Be Obedient

Obedience is where the rubber meets the road. Continuing the above example, obedience is where the "I'm sorry" turns into real-life action and denying self. Being obedient means that not only do you *believe* God knows what's best for you, but you also follow His path. That's when you pray, you ask for God's will to be done, and you actually mean it. Being obedient means applying God's living, breathing Word to your life. It means turning from Jacob to Israel.

It's much harder to be obedient than willing because obedience requires a *true* denial of self. You may be *willing* to live a righteous life, but seem to just somehow never quite get there. Why? Because when you see something you want, you take it. You reach out and grab what gives immediate self-gratification or makes you feel safe according to worldly standards instead of waiting patiently for the promises of God to unfold in your life.

It's much harder to be obedient than willing
because obedience requires a true denial of self.

#ABANDON

But ask yourself: how amazing would your life be if you were willing to examine the inventory of your heart's shelves and throw out those areas where you find yourself living in disobedience?

WHY IS OBEDIENCE SO HARD?

It's really easy to be both willing and obedient when God is answering all your prayers and giving you all the things you want. When you get a new car, a nice big check, or the perfect job, it's easy to praise God and assume you're doing all the right things. But life doesn't usually work that way. So we—willing followers of Christ—say to ourselves, "I don't need to listen for, or be obedient to, what the still soft voice of God is saying. I'm going to pray for (whatever it is your praying for), and if I don't get it from God, I'm just going to go ahead and get it anyway, all on my own."

Or perhaps the situation is like the one we talked about earlier—you have a very prominent job and you earn six figures or more. But every day you feel God prompting you to give a substantial amount of that hard-earned money away to a good cause or, better yet, walk away from the job completely and follow the course He has charted for you. But you're scared. You're scared of losing the respect you get when you answer the ever-present question, "So, what do you do for a living?" You're scared you won't be able to live on a five-figure instead of a six-figure salary, and you don't trust God's will to provide for you in your moment of need.

These are the times obedience is just plain *hard*. This is why Jacob struggled so much with being obedient to God—he felt he wasn't getting what he wanted when he wanted it. The lesson Jacob later learned was that success isn't measured by how much we have gained or acquired. Instead, success is measured by our obedience to what God desires. Sometimes we have to learn this lesson the hard way.

> Success is measured by our obedience
> to what God desires.
>
> #ABANDON

When I was a little boy, my uncle used to cut my hair for me. My uncle had hair on the side of his head, but he was bald in the middle. Unfortunately, I remember thinking that looked so cool, and that I wanted hair just like that. I asked my dad if at my next haircut my uncle could do my hair that way—leave it on the sides, shave it bald in the middle like George Jefferson. Of course my dad said no. But I wouldn't take no for an answer. The next time my uncle cut my hair, I asked him to do my hair just like his. He, too, said no. He told me I'd look crazy. I didn't understand that—I didn't think my uncle looked crazy, so why would I?

I decided to take matters into my own hands. One night when my parents were in the living room, I snuck upstairs to their bathroom and got my dad's clippers. I proceeded to give myself the perfect haircut—shaved bald, right down the middle. As you can imagine, it wasn't the perfect haircut at all, and I realized right away that I had done something pretty awful. I slowly cleaned the hair off of myself and out of the sink, then began the dreaded walk down the steps to the living room, where there was no way I could hide my disobedience from my father. In fact, I wouldn't be able to hide my disobedience from anyone! It was there for all the world to see.

My father took one look at me and burst out laughing. After he finished laughing, I expected full well for him to give me instructions to pick out a belt of my liking for some sort of discipline. But he didn't. Because he knew that wearing that haircut around, day in and day out until all the hair grew back, was punishment enough.

When we get impatient to have things go our way and shun obedience to God to pursue our own path, the enemy steals in. God doesn't then punish us in these moments, but instead lets the natural repercussions of our disobedience happen.

#ABANDON

God treats our indiscretions in the same way. When we get impatient to have things go our way and shun obedience to God to pursue our own path, the enemy steals in. God doesn't then punish us in these moments, but instead lets the natural repercussions of our disobedience happen. To avoid this altogether, we would be well off listening to God, following His rules, and waiting for His blessings to fill our lives. If we don't, we will suffer rather than be filled with the blessings God has in store for us.

Remember—the right way is not *your* way. It is not the *easy* way. It is not the *instant gratification* way. But it is the *abundant* way.

It may be true that the path cut out for you is completely different than the one you imagined. It may be true God is asking you to make some bold, gut-wrenching decisions. Those decisions are scary, especially if you're living an easy life right now. But you must remember that while the task of being you may be difficult at times, it is always necessary— God has great things in store for you. Things that will give your heart and soul fulfillment on a level you never even dreamed possible. It's going to take a real leap of faith to move from *willing* to *obedient*, but I promise you won't be sorry.

> Remember—the right way is not *your* way.
> It is not the *easy* way. It is not the *instant gratification* way. But it is the *abundant* way.
>
> #ABANDON

For thought:

- If you're being honest with yourself, in what areas of your life can you be more obedient to God?

- What are some of those areas in your life you wish God would simply not notice?

- Have you noticed some areas of life where it's your way over God's way?

One place to start to answer that last question is by eliminating the junk and clutter from your life, which is what we'll focus on next.

"You are a rare, one-of-a-kind, valuable, and precious child of God. It's time you started believing that."

#ABANDON

Chapter Two

SOUL JUNKIE

There's no denying that eating too much junk food is bad for us in numerous ways. It's our poor eating habits that eventually lead to terrible health conditions such as diabetes, high blood pressure, high cholesterol, and a long list of other ailments. But as bad as the junk food is for our health, we eat it anyway! Why? Because we love how it tastes!

Far too often we deny the ways that our spiritual life is like our daily diet. Just as we replace fruits, veggies, and whole grains with soda, candy, and fat, we often substitute spiritual food—prayer, Scripture, worshiping in a local church community—with the junk food of the world. We find ourselves "too busy" for daily talks with God and immersion in His Word, skipping church to watch football or sleep in, and then we wonder why we feel soul sick. We feel depressed, lost, quick-tempered, and anxious, to name a few. We pull through drive-thru after drive-thru, wanting the convenience of fries, burgers, and a shake, but disregard the long-term damage inherent in a short-term fix. Perhaps it goes deeper than that. We don't even begin to look for the healthy stuff like communal worship and prayer, but instead ignore our faith altogether or simply take it for granted, or let temptations get the best of us. If any of these things are taking place in your life, it's time to go on a soul-food diet.

When going on a diet, it's important to note where your weak area or areas are. Is it soda? Chocolate? Fried foods? You can't eliminate the empty calories until you figure out where they're coming from. What do you reach for in your moments of weakness? Times of sadness? Or even each day, out of habit and ease? Is it easier to stop at the drive-thru than take the time to plan out a meal? Take some time to think about this and really get a handle on what it is that's causing the problem. Once you identify the junk and cut it out, you might find yourself with a big gap in your menu and dinner planning. No more mid-day snack cakes or loaded potatoes at dinner. But now you find yourself hungry and your plate is looking bare. So how will you choose to fill yourself? Will you replace junk with more junk, or will you turn to what's healthy and wholesome?

In our walk with God, it's no different. We must identify what's taking us from the walk with Christ we desire. Perhaps it's pornography. Or greed. Maybe it's that secret dependency on prescription pills or drugs of some sort. Whatever it is, you have to recognize and name it before you can cut it from your life. And once it's cut, you have to fill the void with something good, something spiritually and soulfully healthy, or else you'll just be left hungry—or worse, tempted by the unspiritual and soulfully unhealthy.

A lot of people diet and achieve a level of success only to once again succumb to temptation, craving, and convenience. This can cause guilt, anger, and shame. You wanted to do better. You gave it your all (or so you think), but failure and junk fillers found you once again. You might be afraid you'll do this same thing once you begin living the life God wants for you. It's all too easy to fall prey to old habits, especially when the entire world seems to be screaming out ways we can find more and more junk to fill our souls, and gives us easier and easier ways to do it. You might be afraid others will see you as hypocritical, and that you'll set a bad example of the Christian life. You might be afraid your spouse will say, "I knew you couldn't stick with it! You'll never change." Repentance is our action and forgiveness is God's reaction out of His perfect love for us. So while it's true that no one is perfect, it's important to remember that God is the King of second chances. And if you're like me, He's the king of the umpteenth chance!

Now get ready to put that hand to good use and take some notes. It's time to get honest and bring those bad habits to the forefront so we, with the help of God, can eliminate them once and for all.

WHAT ARE YOU HUNGRY FOR?

In American society, people are starving, just not for food. The vast majority of Americans don't know about physical hunger and thirst. Being hungry is missing breakfast and having to wait until lunch, and being thirsty is craving anything other than water. Each and every one of us have a spiritual hunger inside of us, but sometimes we can't pinpoint exactly what it is or how we can resolve the matter.

So we use phrases like, "Something is missing from my life," "I'm burned out," "There has to be more to life than what I'm experiencing," and, "Something just isn't right." Even when it seems the cards are falling in our favor and great things are happening, there is still this nagging sensation that…something's missing!

Why is it that so many people are so empty and unsatisfied? The Bible says it's because they're looking in the wrong place. The first place we normally look to be satisfied is through pleasure. *If I could go on vacation… If I could travel the world… If only I could hit the lottery…* The Bible says in Ecclesiastes 1:8, "No matter how much we see, we are never satisfied; no matter how much we hear, we are not content" (TLB). We find this to be all too true when we get up late at night for one of our midnight refrigerator voyages. We don't know exactly what we want, we just know we want something. So we open the refrigerator door, take a bite out of an old sandwich, and put it back only to pick up a slice of cake that also brings no satisfaction. We close the door and head back to our beds, still hungry.

> We don't know exactly what we want,
> we just know we want something.
>
> #ABANDON

Many people are the same way in life, to the point that they'll try anything. They'll abandon the rules and go for what is convenient, and immediate, at that present time. The Bible says that the pleasures of sin last a short time. They simply just don't stay with us (see Hebrews 11:25).

The second place we tend to look for satisfaction is our work.

There is a myth that says, "Success produces satisfaction." But clearly that's not true. Many successful people are noticeably unsatisfied on the inside. After many accomplishments and winning at nearly everything, there comes an emptiness, that feeling that something's just not there. The Bible says that man is always working, never satisfied (see Ecclesiastes 6:7). There are a lot of busy people who get absolutely nothing done. Avoid being one of them by promising yourself you will no longer waste time with the things that don't matter.

Another place we look for satisfaction, which I believe is the most common, is in our possessions. We see "satisfaction guaranteed" on products twice as often today as we did five years ago. Are people twice as happy? Of course not!

> There is a myth that says,
> *"Success produces satisfaction."*
> #ABANDON

Ecclesiastes 5:10 states, "He who loves money will never have enough. The foolishness of thinking wealth brings happiness!" (TLB). The poor people say, "When I get enough money, then all of my problems will be solved."

I can tell you straight out that that no matter what our society tells us, money is just not the answer to happiness. Consider, for instance, the story of Emanuel Ninger. Ninger was an exceptionally talented artist of the late 1800s who was arrested for buying bond paper, cutting it, and turning it into the spitting image of a fifty-dollar bill. Ninger was such a great artist, his counterfeit money fooled anyone and everyone who saw it. But in the end, of course, he was caught.

He was caught because he attempted to pay a bar tab with a counterfeit fifty-dollar bill. The bill got wet on the bar's counter, and the bartender noticed the ink beginning to run and reported Ninger to the police. The police arrested him. Some reports also indicate that Ninger had created three portraits, which were later auctioned off. Each piece of art eventually sold for more than $5,000.00, which, believe it or not, would be close to seven million dollars today.

Ninger had an amazing talent—one that could have made him a millionaire. This was a God-given gift, but Ninger let his good gift go bad, and instead of making millions of dollars creating beautiful artwork, he spent countless hours hand-crafting $50 bills that would eventually land him in jail.

Take Ninger's story as a warning: He let his desire for money rule his life. Just as in his case, the quality of your decisions will determine the quality of your destiny, and if you're letting money and material things determine how you go through life, you will find that you are never quite satisfied with anything.

The quality of your decisions will
determine the quality of your destiny.

#ABANDON

What, then, is the secret of satisfaction?

Psalms 37:4 says "Seek your happiness in the Lord, and He will give you your heart's desire" (GNT). Don't seek happiness, seek God and you will find happiness. Happiness and satisfaction are byproducts of seeking God. If finding happiness and satisfaction are your goals in life, you are going to have a lot of disappointing days ahead. But if you seek God, He will give you the desires of your heart.

JACOB'S EMPTY HEART

While part of Esau's hunger was felt in the true sense of the word, Jacob's was not. Jacob's hunger wasn't in his stomach, but his heart. This hunger came from Jacob's belief that he was "less than."

Genesis 2:7 states that man was created as a "living soul," consisting of the mind (which includes the conscience), the will, and the emotions, and that the soul and the spirit are mysteriously tied together and make up what the Scriptures call the "heart."

There are far too many times that our hunger comes from the belief that we are "less than."

#ABANDON

This is where Jacob's story becomes our own. There are far too many times that our hunger comes from the belief that we are "less than." We are hungry for money, so we act dishonestly to make a quick buck. We are desperate for physical affection, so we make bad decisions in our love lives. We want something new and shiny, so we pull out the credit card to make it ours.

This is because we, like Jacob, are trying to satisfy our soul hunger with *things*. The enemy knows how we long for *things*, and he will use every device he has to tempt us. Wanting more and more and more will pull us in every direction—each turn a wrong turn, each new path the wrong path. Whether it's food, sex, power, money, or even love sought the wrong way, we are too weak to face temptation on our own; we need supernatural strength on our side to say "no" to filling up quick on the junk food we're conveniently handed. We need a constant reminder that the good life isn't about looking good, feeling good, or having the goods. Instead it comes from the one who *is good*. Every single one of us—without the benefit of God on our side—will disregard our gifts and act rashly and without discernment, then beg God to fix the mess we have made.

Thankfully, when we realize the error of our ways and beg for another chance or for God to fix the mess we've made, God is right there, listening.

> We need a constant reminder that the good life isn't about looking good, feeling good, or having the goods. Instead it comes from the one who *is good.*
>
> #ABANDON

Because of the sacrifice Jesus made, you (and I) get a perpetual second chance

Unlike Isaac's limited number of blessings that left Esau wanting more, God's blessings and mercy are abundant beyond our wildest dreams. The story of Jacob demonstrates this very clearly. Jacob wasn't a perfect guy; in fact, he was far from it. He had problems and faults, and he certainly committed his share of sins. But as we have already seen and will continue to see, God loved Jacob and used him for His good work. God sought out Jacob time and again, even though Jacob continued to put God off and walk the walk he wanted, not the walk God wanted. In fact, God was willing to go so far as to rename Jacob twice—Jacob just wasn't ready for it the first time, but God said that was okay. He would give Jacob another chance. This is what makes the story of Jacob so powerful—we are all Jacob. We have faults. We make mistakes. And sometimes, the Lord speaks to us and we take our time in listening. So if God can love and forgive Jacob, giving him chance after chance, God can do the same for us.

JACOB THE DECEIVER
(GENESIS 25:19-34; 27:1-41)

Jacob's early life pattern was one of deceit and of being deceived. He first deceived his brother, then his father and brother both. Jacob then fell victim himself to deceit, when Laban gave him the wrong daughter as a wife. In return, years later, Jacob deceived Laban by masterfully altering the flocks so that Laban would lose his sheep to Jacob.

No doubt about it, Jacob was a skilled, champion deceiver.

Yet, for some reason, God kept talking to Jacob. He continued to advise Jacob how to remain safe and what actions to take. He continued to guide and direct his every turn, even when Jacob railed against God while Esau was coming after him, demanding to know why God had not kept to His word that Jacob would be safe. Even then, God protected him and kept him.

Now, that isn't to say God let Jacob off easy. Not true at all. Instead, Jacob went down a long, meandering life path, losing and gaining, only to lose and gain all over again. Jacob turned to God when times were tough, but we never see Jacob simply praise God in all His goodness—unless God had first bestowed a blessing or miracle upon Jacob, or unless Jacob was in a moment of great need.

We can't accurately determine how God felt about Jacob's back and forth attitude because we're not God. But we do know that God chose to give Jacob a dream in which God spoke to him. We know that God also went out of His way to find Jacob on the banks of the Jabbok and wrestle with him to prove a point. God allowed Jacob to win that wrestling match, but not before he dislocated his hip. I believe God did that as a continual reminder to Jacob and everyone who came into contact with him that he was no longer the same man he once was. He was instead changed forever.

It may seem that Jacob had a slightly more direct connection to God than we do. You know—being sent visions, wrestling with an angel, being renamed by God Himself, not to mention forever walking with a limp as a result. That, however, isn't really the case. We *all* have the same access, the same direct line to God—prayer and the powerful act of listening and discerning. Using this direct line, we can ask that our eyes be open to the junk we're filling our souls with. We can ask for forgiveness, and we can ask that God help us change our ways and begin filling our hearts and souls with righteousness.

BUT HOW?

The first step is probably the hardest—calling out the *what* and *why* of the junk we're filling our souls with. This isn't easy. In fact, it's downright *hard* to take a long, hard, honest look and do personal inventory into our own souls and see what junk is in there, where it came from, and then get it out. It starts with being honest with ourselves. It starts with the hard part first.

What do you find yourself longing for? How do you go about getting those things? Do you find yourself defending your actions? Do you take your desires to God, or are they things you try to hide from Him because you know they aren't the things of righteousness? Do you plead with God to have things your way, right away, or do you ask Him to do His work in you, whatever that may be?

> In fact, God chose to give Jacob a glimpse of the future to let him know that his past did not disqualify him.
>
> #ABANDON

The answers to these questions will tell you if what you're filling up on is good, nutritional soul food, or whether it's soulless cheese puffs, ice cream, and the unhealthy convenience of a soulless drive-thru mentality. It will take some serious self-examination, and more than a little time in prayer and active listening, to be successful in your soul-junk diet. But you *can* be successful.

If you've been filling up on junk for far too long, you may feel too soul-sick to even think about changing your habits. It's certainly easier to throw up your hands than do the roll-up-your-sleeves work of introspection and getting right with God. I'm betting there are a few thoughts running through your head that you want to use as excuses not to do this hard work. Here are a few that cross my mind often:

You're afraid you're too messed up for God to fix.

We know that God accepted Jacob, flaws and all. In fact, God chose to give Jacob a glimpse of the future to let him know that his past did not disqualify him.

I am the Lord God of Abraham your father and the God of Isaac; the land on which you lie I will give to you and your descendants. Also your descendants shall be as the dust of the earth; you shall spread abroad to the west and the east, to the north and the south; and in you and in your seed all the families of the earth shall be blessed. Behold, I am with you and will keep you wherever you go, and will bring you back to this land; **for I will not leave you until I have done what I have spoken to you** (Genesis 28:14 NKJV).

Getting right with God—really *right*—
stirs up a desire from somewhere deep
inside to walk the righteous walk.

#ABANDON

Many years passed after Jacob received this dream. Throughout that time, there were good years and there were bad ones. There were times when Jacob sought out God, but for the most part he didn't. He demanded safe passage from God, but did little in return. Nonetheless, there on the banks of the Jabbok, many, many years after Jacob dreamed about the ladder going into Heaven and heard the direct voice of God, God held good to His word. He changed Jacob to Israel, and Jacob went from being a deceiver, thief, and liar to being a prince, and God enabled Jacob to pass his inheritance down to his grandsons.

The Good News is, God can and will do the same for you. Grace abounds, no less for you than for others. Does grace make all the stuff we have said about hard work and change null and void? Definitely not. Getting right with God—really *right*—stirs up a desire from somewhere deep inside to walk the righteous walk. It's the junk of the world combined with human nature that gets in your way and keeps you from following that desire. And when that desire is all misconstrued or lacking, so too is your life.

> Your only limitations are the
> ones you give yourself.
>
> #ABANDON

The point here is that living righteously and finally having the fulfillment you've wanted both come from being content right where you are with just what you've got. Your only limitations are the ones you give yourself; if you let Him, God will continue to fill you up with so much good and abundance that it will crowd out all those other things you've been filling up on over the years.

You're afraid you can't change.

I love to shop online. I always have. Once, many years ago, I ordered an expensive gadget from eBay that I was really excited about getting. This was back when eBay was still sketchy, at best, and it was a "buyer beware" sort of place. Nonetheless, I took my chances and ordered this gadget. As the days mounted, I looked forward more and more to its arrival, but after two weeks it had yet to arrive. I emailed the seller, who responded by sending me the tracking number. I followed the tracking, but the package had yet to arrive. Finally, after about three weeks, the package arrived. I was so excited, I immediately tore the box open, right there in the doorway. After wrestling with the tape and the packing peanuts, I looked inside, where I found…bricks. And a towel.

I wasted no time in emailing the seller, who pointed out to me that his eBay terms said absolutely *no* returns or refunds under any circumstances. He had tricked me by giving me something I didn't ask for, didn't want, and hadn't bargained for. And worse, there was nothing I could do to fix it. (By the way, eBay now has strict policies in place to prevent this, and they require honesty from their sellers. They also enforce their rules in order to protect their buyers and sellers.)

In life we often receive things that don't really belong to us and aren't what we asked for, wanted, or bargained for. These things come from the enemy, but sometimes we fail to see that. Instead, we take on the thing like it actually belongs to us, no returns or refunds allowed.

Thankfully, this isn't how it works with God. God has empowered us to reject these unwanted packages—to put them right back in the mailbox, labeled "return to sender," and never have to see them again. It's up to you—will you hold on to what the enemy has forced into your life, or will you label it "return to sender" at the first chance you get? It's true that no one is perfect, but as a child of God you have strength to fight the temptation beckoning to you from every corner of your life. You have the tools—prayer, the Bible, church, community—it's up to you to decide whether or not you're willing to use those tools to help you live fully and "send back" to the enemy all the sneaky ways he tries to bring you down.

> God has empowered us to reject
> these unwanted packages.
>
> #ABANDON

Of course, it's very seldom that full change takes place overnight. You're going to have to do some hard work and go through some struggles before you get to the place you want to be—living the good life as a changed person. It may have become a popular saying and a bit cliché, but it is still so true—all things are possible through Christ (see Philippians 4:13). That means it's even possible for you—sinner, soul junkie, and mere mortal—to exchange your old diet for a brand new, healthy, nutritious, and virtuous one that would be the envy of any fitness buff.

You may be afraid you'll change, but then just go right back to your old diet of junk.

You can't stumble over what's behind you.

Later in the book we'll talk about the importance of having an escape route to keep you from backsliding into your old diet. Spoiler alert: that escape route includes some key tools, especially having a daily devotional time, prayer, worshiping in community, accountability, and surrounding yourself with the things of a righteous life. With these tools, your odds of diet failure are greatly reduced. But the burden is indeed on you to keep up the good habits that will strengthen your spirit and resolve and keep you from straying from the path you've worked so hard to get on.

There will undoubtedly be some bumps and bruises along the way—remember Jacob's hip?—but you can't let that stop you. And don't worry—if you're still afraid that you can't do this whole life of righteousness thing, and if you still don't quite trust that God will come through for you, the next chapter has you covered.

You can't stumble over what's behind you.
#ABANDON

For thought:

- What are you hungry for?
- How are you currently feeding your hunger in a godly way?
- Do you feel like you aren't good enough for God?

Spend some time at the end of your day thinking and praying on these things. Realize that God loves you and wants you just as you are. Give your heart and life wholly to Him and He will do an amazing work in and through you.

"Repentance is our action and forgiveness is God's reaction out of His perfect love for us."

#ABANDON

Chapter Three

DITCH THE DOUBT

Doubt is a silent assassin that has the ability to suck the life out of any thought, dream, or vision if we allow it to. I have learned over time that doubt kills more dreams than failure ever will. Feeling doubt isn't rare or unique; in fact, all of us, at some point in our lives, will be faced with doubt of one type or another. Doubt can take many different forms. Some of us may go through periods when we doubt the existence of God. For others, it's doubt about whether or not God is truly involved in our lives. A common doubt is about God's goodness, given the sorry and fallen state of the world we live in.

> Doubt is a silent assassin that has the ability to suck the life out of any thought, dream, or vision if we allow it to.
>
> #ABANDON

I know you might think that I, as a pastor, as a person who grew up with godly parents who preached the word of God worldwide, have never experienced doubt. You may even think I judge you for having doubts, and think I can't understand what that's like. But I promise you, I know doubt all too well. I have had many situations in my life that led me to doubt. There's one story in particular that comes to mind when I think of times that led me away from God.

When I was about twelve years old, my father and I were at a shopping center in Los Angeles and decided to sit down for a quick lunch. He and I both loved hot dogs (in our minds, we were world-class hot dog connoisseurs), so that's what we decided to eat. As we sat down to take our first bites, an odd thing happened: my father couldn't open his mouth wide enough to eat. My first thought was lockjaw, but my father asked me to massage his neck, and after that massage he was able to eat. So clearly he didn't have lockjaw, but what, then, was causing this odd problem?

From that point forward, this problem only grew worse, and it was clear that something—who knew what—was affecting my father's throat. He and my mom went to the doctor and were told that their hectic traveling schedule was causing the problem. My parents preached nearly five times a week in various cities. They were known worldwide and were on television seven days a week, preaching the gospel. This was my father's very life. Nonetheless, he listened to the doctor and slowed down his traveling schedule. The pain and throat issues, however, did not improve. In fact, they grew worse.

My father, still not understanding what was going on, went to an ear, nose, and throat specialist. That doctor put a scope down his throat to see what was going on, and that very moment became the point that would forever change our lives. The ENT told my father he needed to check himself into a hospital *immediately* for surgery. My father had a tumor the size of a chipmunk in his throat—he had terminal stage four cancer. My father underwent the eight-hour surgery and countless rounds of chemo but was still only given weeks to live.

Now I never saw my dad do any wrong. He never yelled, never smoke, never drank. He was the epitome of being Christ-like and preached the Word of God far and wide. He set the precedent for replicating Jesus. It didn't make sense to me; how could God allow this to happen? In my ignorance, I began to doubt God. I watched my father go from 6 feet 4 inches, 280 pounds, to 6 feet 4 inches, 170 pounds. During the surgery, they had to remove part of his tongue, and from that point forward my father couldn't eat or drink with his mouth. He was fed a liquid diet through a tube placed in his stomach. Despite his discomfort and what seemed to many to be his life wasting away, he steadfastly preached the Word of God. As he began to worsen, he became so weak that I eventually had to dress him, but on Sundays, after I put his clothes on him, he would go to church and preach. *He never stopped preaching*—he wasn't about to let anyone tell him that the hand he was dealt meant he couldn't play.

Despite the example of my father's faith, my doubt grew. I doubted the very existence of God. I became a prodigal son, living for myself and rebelling against the ways in which I was raised. I totally abandoned all I had previously known and lived a life removed from Christ. I couldn't help but wonder—if my Christ-like father could be hit with such a disease, then what did God have in store for me, with all my many flaws? I didn't stand a chance.

For years my father was in and out of the hospital. Even though he couldn't eat or drink, he sat at the family table every night for dinner, just to be near us. He continued to preach and remain firm in his faith. One night I asked him why God would allow this to happen to him, a person who clearly was following the will of God in every way. My father made clear to me that the throat cancer was not from God, but rather from the enemy, attacking my father in the very way he spread the gospel—through preaching, using his tongue and throat—because the enemy did not want my father to continue in his work.

When I was eighteen, my father sat me down for a talk. He told me what it would take to be a real man. Thinking back to it now, it reminds me of the Old Testament practice of a father sitting down with the firstborn son, offering his blessing and passing down the birthright. We talked for *five hours*. When we were done, my father went to bed.

That same night my mother woke me at 2:00 A.M. to tell me my father was incoherent and unresponsive. We called the EMT, but before they arrived my father passed from this world to Heaven.

I knew then that I had to step up and be the man I was raised to be. I may have had my doubts, but my father never did. And through his faith, my faith grew. My doubt turned into a miracle as I thought of my father, cancer-free, enjoying the splendor of Heaven. The faith of my father laid the groundwork for my faith. He never told me to not talk about doubt or feelings. Instead, he said to give those doubts and feelings to God, and to watch as He turned them into miracles. And so He has.

It's what you do when you're faced with doubt that will determine how quickly that doubt disappears.

#ABANDON

You may be in your moment of doubt right now. If so, I'm so glad you're here with me, reading this book and hearing my story. It is imperative that we hold on to this truth—no matter what the doubt is that you might be struggling with, *it's what you do when you're faced with doubt that will determine how quickly that doubt disappears.*

In order for you to come out the other side of doubt stronger than you were before, you have to start by being honest and acknowledging that there is doubt present in your life, then pinpointing where that doubt came from. You can try to deny it and pretend it doesn't exist. You can even try to bury your past doubts—but it doesn't work, trust me. If your doubt remains alive, even pushed down low, it will surely resurrect itself. Just about the time you think it's buried, the doubt will creep back into your mind, quite often at the most inappropriate time. Denying doubt does not relieve doubt. It is only when we present our doubts to

God that we're able to see the miracle He preforms in and through our lives.

Doubt is oftentimes born of low esteem or questioning self-worth. For instance, doubting that God could love anyone with as many faults as you have. Or thinking that God is only there for those who actively pursue righteousness, not those who actively pursue comfort over obedience. For some, something bad has happened, or maybe it's just the dark, depressing nature of the evening news that has you wondering about things. For others, it may be their family of origin and how they were raised.

> Denying doubt does not relieve doubt.
> It is only when we present our doubts to
> God that we're able to see the miracle
> He preforms in and through our lives.
>
> #ABANDON

Other times, doubt comes from not wondering "if," but wondering "when." We can often find ourselves firm in our faith and our belief in God's goodness, but we have reached a season of wondering when all that goodness will enter our life. We sit around, looking up at the sky, waiting for it to open wide. We ask God, "God, just *exactly* when will the new job come through? The soul mate be found? The child conceived? The money made?"

When answers don't immediately show up at a speed second only to that of a Google search, we're immediately flooded with the impatience of a thousand rivers, weighed down by the anxiety and concern of our current situation, and we find ourselves with our heads tilted to the side, not only waiting, but wondering if we will hear God's immediate answer stream down from Heaven. But of course, the sky remains closed and no answer comes—for now. Life is a waiting game most of the time, and I think God intended it that way.

Most of the time when I'm waiting on God, He's really waiting on me. He was ready to give the answer a long time ago, but I wasn't ready to receive it. He's saying, "Grow up! Get some spiritual depth in your life. I want to bless your life, but you can't handle the blessing I want to pour on you at this moment. What I have in store for you is so great, but you're not quite ready to handle this level of blessing." Just because we pray and ask for God's answer doesn't mean we're ready to hear it or accept, and God knows He better wait until just the right time for letting the fruit of our blessings come to bear. God knew He needed to wait to bring Jacob's prophetic blessing into being until Jacob could confess his name and deceitful nature to the Lord; until then, Jacob would not be strong enough to carry forth the blessing. It was only after Jacob confessed his identity to God that Jacob was able to offer reparation to Esau, demonstrating that Jacob was now comfortable with who he was—who God made him to be—rather than struggling to be like someone else.

It's all too easy to trust God when things are going right, but it's much harder to trust Him when things are going wrong or when the thing you're waiting for just seems…to… never…come. Think of waiting as a faith exercise, strengthening your heart, mind, and soul, teaching it to hold tight to the will of God instead of self or world. And perhaps more importantly, hold *loosely* to the things you're waiting—and waiting, and waiting—to have happen. It may be that those aren't the things God intends for you after all (more about that later!).

> Most of the time when I'm waiting on God, He's really waiting on me.
>
> #ABANDON

There are some more "typical" things folks tend to wait for—true love or the perfect job. Others are unique to our own life situation, such as the health of a sick child or watching a parent battle Alzheimer's. Regardless, it is rare that a person never has to wait for something, no matter what it is. Author Joyce Meyer agrees. She writes, "Waiting is a given—we are going to wait. The question is, are we going to wait the wrong or right way?"[1] I say that, given all the things in life we wait for, it's probably best that we learned to wait the *right* way.

But what, exactly, *is* the right way?

LEARNING TO WAIT

To fully answer that question, we have to start by understanding that patience is a *skill,* and one we know Jacob, for a time, completely lacked. I assume there are some people who are just born patient, but I've yet to meet any of them.

Instead, patience is usually developed through tough, frustrating, or otherwise negative life situations. It's really no different than strengthening our muscles. For that to happen, we have to go through some things that are not comfortable to get the results we desire, with many repetitions. Great, right? Who wants to be told that an all-important virtue can only come from some type of suffering, and even from going through trials time and again? Part of learning to wait the right way, however, is learning to understand that "suffering" may not be suffering at all! Your mind probably just said, "Wait, what? *Huh?*" I understand that may not make good logical sense right now, but keep reading as we get into the meat of how this is possible.

I remember vividly as a very young boy going to a recreational facility with my best friend and his father to learn how to swim.

As my friend's father was explaining the dos and don'ts of swimming, I became distracted, watching the other kids running and diving in the swimming pool like the 18-time Olympic gold medalist, Michael Phelps. I could only imagine how fast I would swim for the very first time, and how long it would take me to go from one end of the pool's cool, clear water to the other. There was only one problem—I had impatiently rushed my way through the listening process, nodding my head up and down, signaling yes to every question he asked, but I wasn't really listening. When it came time for us get in, my friend looked at me, smiled, and dove in. He had listened to every word his father had said. His technique was impeccable. He screamed from the pool, "Come on, Tim!

Jump in!" Not to be outdone by my friend, I mustered up the courage, ran, and dove in and…immediately sank to the bottom of the pool like a large stone dipped in iron. As badly as I wanted to swim, I couldn't even remember what to do to get back to the surface. I rushed the instructional process, and I paid the price for it.

Just as I did that day at the pool so long ago, many of us have rushed the process of listening thoroughly to the instructions God has laid out for us. And many have paid some costly prices for it. What we must realize is that the investment in our preparation determines the quality of our performance. Early steps might bore you, but miss even one and you might not get the chance to execute on the later ones. I was embarrassed that day at the pool. And I was upset I had wasted a good swimming lesson and would have to come back again another day. But for all my disappointment and embarrassment, something good came from that low moment: I learned the importance of listening to instruction and of being patient while listening to the rules so I could have fun once I learned to execute those rules.

Knowing that a negative life situation is helping you build a good character trait may not make you feel any happier in the moment, but if we're going to learn the right way to wait, the first step is to jump right in to tough situations. Let me explain that in a little more detail. I am *not* saying to bring negative situations on yourself. Absolutely not. But when they come up—and they will come up!—enter into that season of your life with an attitude of joy, peace, and gratefulness. Remember, if something doesn't challenge you, it won't change you. Be grateful that even in moments of trial God is shaping us, growing us, nurturing us, *changing* us. This is not just me making up some crazy talk; in Romans 5:3 we read that we should not just *accept* tribulation, but that we should take *glory* in it, knowing that God will use that time to teach us patience.

> What we must realize is that the investment in our preparation determines the quality of our performance.
>
> #ABANDON

In fact, this is an idea that is found repeatedly throughout the Bible. The Bible even tells us to *rejoice* in our low moments, using them to relish and roll around in, in the hope that we have through Jesus Christ and the glorious will of God (see Romans 12:12). James 1:2 seems to imply that we should even accept trials as something like a gift: "Consider it pure joy, my brothers and sisters, whenever you face trials of many kinds" (NIV).

We never see Jacob actually *rejoicing* in his trials, but we do see that he learned from them. When his learning was finally complete, he was no longer "Jacob," the man who struggled with his brother Esau; he is instead "Israel," a man who has struggled with God and God has won his soul. This reflects that Jacob had finally learned that in his sinful nature, he was putting power and glory over God as well as his family.

If something doesn't challenge
you, it won't change you.

#ABANDON

Jacob did not learn this because of his own internal strength or greatness. In fact, we read in Hosea that when Jacob struggled with the angel and prevailed, Jacob tearfully begged God to favor him. He could cheat his brother, his father, and his father-in-law, but he couldn't cheat God. All he could do was learn from the lesson God was trying to teach him through trials and tribulations. Jacob's struggle was the fight of faith. He didn't cheat or despair, but rather learned to keep clinging to God in faith, believing that God rewards those who diligently trust in Him even though they are conscious of their weaknesses and would otherwise fail without the help of God. He learned to hold fast to God from that day on.

Learning from his struggles made all the difference in the world for Jacob's development and eventual ability to live a contented life, as well as to bless his grandsons in fulfillment of God's word to him, both of whom went on to father nations (see Genesis 48). This could not have happened if Jacob had not learned to rely on God and grown through the trials he was handed.

So you have now read that you should be *grateful* for trials, as well as take *glory* in them, *rejoice* in them, and even joyfully accept them as gifts. God has nothing if not a sense of humor. I don't know about you, but it is certainly not when I'm down and out that I feel grateful, glorious, or joyful. But note what else God tells us to do during life's rough spots—*to remain in constant prayer* (see Romans 12:12). I know I do this…well, for the most part.

When something happens in life that I don't like or that is particularly hard or stressful for me, I stay in constant prayer, asking God to make things right again. Mostly this means I ask God to fix things to my liking. I go through all the possible acceptable scenarios with God. "Now God," I say, "If this can happen over here, then I can do that over there, and all will be well. So, abracadabra—get to it!" I don't really say that last bit, of course, but God knows that in my heart I pretty much feel that way. God becomes a sort of ATM for dispensing instant fixes, and the wheels in my head turn and turn, weighing options and paths.

I don't think this is what the author of Romans had in mind when he suggested we remain in constant prayer. Our heavenly petitions may not rush God into doing things before He is ready, but they *will* keep us in fellowship with Him.

DEAL OR NO DEAL?

I'm sure every person on God's green earth has done this. You hit a rough patch or *really* want something, and you pray, "God, if You can just make this happen for me, I promise I'll go to church every Sunday/give all my money back to You when I get it," or whatever the case may be. Let me ask you this: has that ever worked for you?

Our heavenly petitions may not rush God into doing things before He is ready, but they *will* keep us in fellowship with Him.

#ABANDON

After Jacob awoke from his wonderful, God-given dream of a ladder reaching from Heaven to earth, with angels running the length of it, Jacob was awash with wonder. And in his wonder, he prayed:

Surely the Lord is in this place, and I did not know it. If God will be with me, and keep me in this way that I am going, and give me bread to eat and clothing to put on, so that I come back to my father's house in peace, then the Lord shall be my God (Genesis 28:16,20-21 NKJV).

What did Jacob do here? Look at his seemingly worshipful words again and what do you find? You'll find a whole bunch of "ifs." *If* God will be with me. *If* God will keep me. *If* God will give me food and clothes. *If* God will give me peace. *If* God will do all these things, then I shall worship Him.

I suppose that's a better option than just ignoring God altogether or denying His existence, but let me be one among many to tell you: God doesn't make deals. No, He gives you a certain hand and you play it to the best of your ability. There's no folding or cheating allowed, and there's no bartering one action for another. Rather, you have to ante up and go all in to what God gives you and worship

Him and be thankful for your hand, no matter what it is. I guarantee God will have you come out on top.

JACOB DECEIVED

There are times when, before we can rise to the top, we have to struggle at the bottom. This is usually the case when we fail to take our confessions to God and ask Him for forgiveness. Without repentance, our sins always come back to get us in the end. And when those have been sins against another, they usually come back to us in the same way we dished them out. This is not a punishment from God, but rather the natural result that occurs from our actions and choices. (Remember my haircut?)

But even in moments when we're given the natural repercussions of our sinful actions, God is still working toward the ends He has planned.

When Jacob asked Laban for Rachel's hand in marriage, Laban didn't make things easy. Laban made Jacob go through some blood, sweat, and tears to get the hand of his daughter, assigning Jacob to seven years of backbreaking work. Then at the end of those seven years, Laban changed his mind. Or, more likely, he had deceit in mind all along. Note, though, that Jacob did not spend time arguing with Laban when Laban said Jacob had to work seven more years before he could marry Rachel. Instead, Jacob went through some quick calculations in his head and figured he could make the best of it. He wasn't going to sacrifice the love of his life because Laban had chosen to deceive him. Instead, Jacob and Laban struck another deal.

Now this doesn't sound fair at all to me. I would have been quite upset with Laban over this whole thing, and might not have handled it as well as Jacob did. No, I think I would have had a thing or two to say to Laban all right. But Jacob was a smart and conniving man; he wasn't going to take no for an answer, but was instead willing to fight—or work—for what he wanted.

He took what he was dealt and he played the game. It wasn't easy, but he eventually won. Jacob suffered the repercussions of his own deceitful actions by becoming the deceived, thus learning his lesson the hard way—we never see Jacob deceive anyone again. We also see that while Jacob had to work hard, God kept to the course He had charted, and Jacob did indeed receive Rachel's hand in marriage.

This just goes to show you that things don't always go our way or according to our timetables. And sometimes they don't even seem "fair." But God is good and God provides, and far be it from us to say what the right way is to go about it. Instead, when we accept the hand we are dealt and do the best we can with it, we will always come out on top.

FORGET FIGURING IT OUT

Another common option for people in low moments is neglecting God altogether and relying on self-directed actions to "get things done." Why make a deal when you can do it yourself, right?

This is what Apostle Paul meant in Romans when he advised us to remain in constant prayer during our greatest times of need—not to pray our way out of our troubles or to handle our troubles all by ourselves, but to give those troubles to God to do with what He will (and trust me, He will!). Paul had plenty of his own ups and downs in life, so I think he knew a thing or two about what he was talking about.

This doesn't mean that you stop looking for answers or give up trying to fix things. God didn't make us passive people who sit on the couch waiting for God to lift our marionette strings and carry us where we need to be. We must work hand and hand with God by applying the following ways of life:

1. Stop relying on yourself for answers.

2. Ditch whatever doubts you have about God and His ability to make things right for you.

3. Pray. You give your troubles to God, ask for His help, and then do that thing we so often forget about—you *listen*.

Proverbs 16:9 says, "A man's heart deviseth his way: but the Lord directeth his steps." In case that wasn't clear enough, we read in Proverbs 20:24 that "Man's goings are of the Lord; how can a man then understand his own way?" In other words, God has already chosen where we need to go and when and how we'll get there. When we fight the perfect will of God, we will find stress, anxiety, misery, and confusion. Our lives will become cluttered and chaotic as we attempt to chart our own course. Or sometimes, we just plain fail, like I did that day at the swimming pool so many years ago. That's because Jesus said that when we live apart from Him, we can do nothing (see John 15:5).

ABANDON

When we call Jesus our Lord and Savior, we are to give our *whole* lives to Him. That doesn't mean we get all the good stuff—like grace and Heaven—but live how we want to here on earth. *It means the entirety of who we are abides in Christ.* We cannot be independent of Him or live separate from Him and expect His fruit to come to bear in our lives.

Keep in mind that "God resisteth the proud, and giveth grace to the humble" (1 Peter 5:5) Trying to solve things on your own, apart from God is a proud action—it's saying that *you*, not God, know what's best. As promised, God will set Himself against that attitude, just as He did with Jacob. But when we walk humbly with God—giving our whole selves to Him, trusting Him, and not making a single decision without Him—that is when the fullness of God's grace will abound in our lives.

> We cannot be independent of Him or live separate from Him and expect His fruit to come to bear in our lives.
> #ABANDON

We can't use what we think we know in our heads to judge where our lives are going and how we're going to get there. Instead we have to open ourselves to the gift of not needing to know all the answers in our timing. We must look for what God is revealing to us and trust that things will happen the right way and in His perfect time.

THE KEY WORD IS TRUST

By the time Jacob left Laban's to return home, Jacob seemed to have developed trust in God. But when Jacob encountered the problem of Esau coming to meet him in the desert, Jacob's trust began to falter:

> *Then Jacob said, "O God of my father Abraham and God of my father Isaac, the Lord who said to me, 'Return to your country and to your family, and I will deal well with you': I am not worthy of the least of all the mercies and of all the truth which You have shown Your servant; for I crossed over this Jordan with my staff, and now I have become two companies. Deliver me, I pray, from the hand of my brother, from the hand of Esau; for I fear him, lest he come and attack me and the mother with the children. For You said, 'I will surely treat you well, and make your descendants as the sand of the sea, which cannot be numbered for multitude'"* (Genesis 32:9-12 NKJV).

Now Jacob did the right thing by taking his worries to God, but do you see what else Jacob did here? He tried to passively aggressively sweet talk God. He praised Him, then asked for something (safety), then essentially said, "You better give me what I'm asking for because You already promised it to me!" And, of course, God did indeed keep His promise, but not because Jacob tried sweet talking Him!

Even when we begin to discern God's plan for us, we, like Jacob, can feel scared or unsure of ourselves. We may notice our lives are going well and that we're feeling confident about the direction we're headed, then all of a sudden we pull back in uncertainty, doubt, and fear. The enemy sees that we are doing the Lord's work, so he steals in and hands us doubt. We find ourselves thinking things like, "Who, me? God is going to use *me* for *that*? I'm not good enough/strong enough/smart enough for that!" Or, "God will truly do that work in my life?" Our trust flags, and we start doubting the signs of God's hand that we see all around us and questioning whether what we're hearing is really the true voice of the Lord or just our own wishful thinking and imagination.

Proverbs 3:5-6 says, "Lean on, trust in, and be confident in the Lord with all your heart and mind and do not rely on your own insight or understanding. In all your ways know, recognize, and acknowledge Him, and He will direct and make straight and plain your paths" (AMP).

In other words, *God does not respond to you by the situation you are dealing with, but by the ability you possess to trust Him in the midst of the situation*. Believe that what God has created for you, you shall accomplish, no matter what your current situation is.

Believe what God has told you to do, and success will follow. What you must continue to do is put one foot in front of the other and God will continue to unfold the path before you one step at a time. You may not be able to see around every bend in the road, but God knows what's on the other side. Your destiny is God's history; spend time with Him to uncover and discover His desired path for your life.

God does not respond to you by the situation you are dealing with, but by the ability you possess to trust Him in the midst of the situation.

#ABANDON

During all moments, remember that God causes things to happen at exactly the right time, and that good moments become good memories and bad moments become good lessons. Your job is not to figure out when or how, but to make up your mind that you won't give up until you cross the finish line and are living in the radical, outrageous blessings of God. The more you trust Jesus and keep your eyes focused on Him, the more abundant life you will have. Trusting God brings life and believing brings rest. So stop trying to figure everything out, and let God be God in your life.

Pray these things as you commit yourself to ditching doubt on a daily basis:

- That God would remove your doubt;

- That God would replace that doubt with hope;

- That God would speak to your heart, strengthen your faith, and restore your soul.

NOTE

1. Joyce Meyer, "When God's Timing Is Taking Too Long," Joyce Meyer Ministries, Wait with Patience, accessed October 14, 2014, http://www.joycemeyer.org/articles/ea.aspx?article=when_gods_timing_is_taking_too_long.

"It's what you do when you're faced with doubt that will determine how quickly that doubt disappears."

#ABANDON

Phase Two

THE CHALLENGE

In Phase One, we addressed righteousness and abandoning our lives to Jesus. That's great, but even the most righteous, most abandoned-to-Jesus person will encounter temptation. It doesn't do us any good to pretend that we are never tempted—even Jesus was tempted!

When Jesus was tempted, He didn't *ignore* Satan and try to pretend he didn't exist. Instead, He faced him head on and told him how it was going to be. That's exactly the type of courage we must face temptation with! The more we try to belittle and play down the temptation, the more it will eat away at us. Instead of trying to hide it or hide from it, we need to own it, take responsibility for it, face it head on, and tell it how it's going to be. We know that darkness is here with us and will entice us to succumb to unrighteousness and sinful actions. Our role as a believer of Christ is to *resist* those forces of darkness. So how do we make sure we can do that?

By having an escape route.

> The more we try to belittle and play down the temptation, the more it will eat away at us.
>
> #ABANDON

In this section of the book we're going to get you set up, map and all, with the steps you need to take to ensure spiritual safety in the face of temptation. The good thing is that—like typical fire escapes and evacuation plans—God has given us the tools we need to get out of any tempting situation we may be faced with. Our number one tool is the Word of God, better known as the Bible. Every situation you can ever imagine is in the Bible. You may find that hard to believe—and some may say it *was* written a long time ago—but trust me, the Word of God is a living, breathing thing that applies to our lives as much today as it did way back in the beginning of time.

Another tool is communicating with God through prayer. If someone breaks into your house, the first thing you would most likely do after you are in a secure location is pick up the phone, call 911, and the police would be at your doorstep in no time. So why is it when the enemy breaks into our daily lives and interrupts our thought patterns that we neglect to call our spiritual authority? When it comes to the devil's wily ways, we can always use our direct line to God—prayer—and He'll give us the instruction, along with the courage, we need in order to overcome every time.

We will also learn how to take the things you read in this section and add them to your exit strategy, giving you a supernaturally charged tool kit to fight temptation, selfishness, low self-esteem, and doubt. The enemy doesn't play around, and he'll do whatever it takes to keep us down and focused on all the bad things in life. God wants just the opposite for us; He wants us to be full of joy and confidence, knowing that He will provide a way of escape.

Chapter Four

ABANDON YOUR WAYS

TEMPTATION

It's no exaggeration when I say we have all been tempted at one time or another. Temptation is anything that tries to influence or seduce us into disobedience—it is something even Jesus faced. Hebrews 4:15 tells us that Jesus "was in all points tempted like as we are, yet without sin." He overcame the temptations with, among other things, fasting and prayer. In Matthew, we read the account of Jesus's temptation:

Then Jesus was led by the Spirit into the wilderness to be tempted by the devil. After fasting forty days and forty nights, he was hungry. The tempter came to him and said, "If you are the Son of God, tell these stones to become bread."

Jesus answered, "It is written: 'Man shall not live on bread alone, but on every word that comes from the mouth of God.'"

Then the devil took him to the holy city and had him stand on the highest point of the temple. "If you are the Son of God," he said, "throw yourself down. For it is written: 'He will command his angels concerning you, and they will lift you up in their hands, so that you will not strike your foot against a stone.'"

Jesus answered him, "It is also written: 'Do not put the Lord your God to the test.'"

Again, the devil took him to a very high mountain and showed him all the kingdoms of the world and their splendor. "All this I will give you," he said, "if you will bow down and worship me."

Jesus said to him, "Away from me, Satan! For it is written: 'Worship the Lord your God, and serve him only.'"

Then the devil left him, and angels came and attended him (Matthew 4:1-11 NIV).

Remember, it's not the temptation itself that is sin; the real problem is *giving in* to the temptation.

#ABANDON

Temptations in our own lives are inevitable. You are going to be tempted. The more you grow toward the Lord, the greater the temptation is. Pretending it doesn't exist in our daily lives will only limit us and our ability to allow God to strengthen the vulnerable areas of our lives. Remember, it's not the temptation itself that is sin; the real problem is *giving in* to the temptation.

What you risk reveals what you value.

#ABANDON

You have to be ready, willing, and able to fight against the enemy when temptation comes your way. It will be in the very moment you relax that temptation will come into your life—don't let it catch you unaware. Instead, do two things to protect yourself. The first thing you have to do is place boundaries between you and the things that might cause you to fall deeper into the trap of temptation. If you know a particular situation, person, or thing will cause temptation to invade your life, avoid those situations, people, and things. Don't tell yourself you're strong enough to fight temptation on your own if it comes your way. What you risk reveals what you value. You may not actually be *doing* the thing that's tempting you, but you sure are thinking about it! Eventually, the thinking may become action. What you think about long enough, you will do. Think about this: Two grizzly bears get into a fight. They are the same weight, height, and strength. They have the same disposition and they both have the willpower to fight to the end.

Which will win?

The one that eats the most. What's interesting is that our flesh and Spirit are very similar and are at war with each other every day. Whichever you feed the most is going to win.

Why take the chance? Follow the great advice given in Jude 1:20 to build "yourselves up on your most holy faith, praying in the Holy Spirit," and set up the necessary boundaries to cut it off before it can take root.

The second thing we should implement is spiritual protection by having a strong exit strategy.

Whichever you feed the most is going to win.

#ABANDON

EXIT STRATEGIES

In July of 2012, my family and I lost our home to a fire. I can remember that day as if it were yesterday. It was a beautiful Sunday afternoon. We came home from church, changed our clothes, and began to relax as my mother prepared lunch in the kitchen. The relaxation quickly came to an end, however, when we heard an explosion toward the back of the house coming from the porch. My mother and I tried frantically to put out the flames from what seemed to be a faulty propane tank on the left side of the house.

As hard as we tried, nothing could quench the flames that were quickly engulfing our home and all that was in it. We soon realized nothing we could physically do would help, and that we were in danger of losing our lives. Once in the driveway, my mom realized one of her dogs was still inside, and that there was no way he could get himself out or survive the fire.

I knew that if I went back in to get the dog that my odds of getting out of the house alive, or at the very least unharmed, were slim. But my mom was panicking and her breaking heart over the sure loss of her dog spurred me to action. My first thought of having to run into a burning house was not a pleasant one, and surely not something I wanted to do. However, I decided to act against my own desire to stay safe outside the house, and attempt my own search and rescue for my mother's dog. I pushed and scrambled my way through the smoke and the flames that had almost instantly filled the house. Eventually, after crawling through three rooms, I found the dog cowering in a corner. I'm not sure who was more scared at this point—me or the dog! When I tried to pick him up, he was so incredibly panicked that instead of leaping into my arms at the chance of rescuing, he reacted defensively and bit my wrist. At this point, almost faint from breathing smoke, I quickly grabbed the dog and got him out of the house by any means necessary. As I pushed my way back through the smoke and flames with watery eyes and smoke-filled lungs, burning wood began to fall on my back. Scared for my life, I ran as fast as I could through an open path that I saw.

By all accounts, there is no way I should have made it out with just the few minor injuries and burns I got that day.

But I did. God provided an escape route for me, and just as God provided a path or escape route for me in a burning house, He will provide a way of escape for you when you need him most.

Any building that abides by a fire code will have a fire escape plan to use in case of emergency. Some buildings will even have tools to go along with the plan, such as defibrillators, fire extinguishers, and heavy things to "smash glass in case of emergency." There are maps on the walls with little stars (you are here!) and arrows pointing you to the closest escape route if there is a fire or some other type of calamity.

Thanks to these fire codes, we understand that if an emergency situation arises, we have an exit strategy. You won't have to logic your way out of a dangerous situation. Perhaps you won't be calm, cool, and collected, but someone else has already done the hard work of designating an emergency plan for you; all you have to do is follow it.

During our times of temptation, doubt, and weakness, we, too, need an escape route. When you're thinking about doing something that you know isn't to the glory of God and is far from the good referenced in Philippians 4:8, you need a plan in place. Without one, it'll be hard to say no to the temptation that is presented to you.

Jacob was often at risk of losing his way, and each time he started to get a little lost, God entered into his life directly to reorient Jacob. Most importantly, perhaps, was when God appeared to Jacob in a dream of a ladder running from Heaven to earth. God used this ladder to reach down to Jacob and promise that no matter where Jacob wandered,

God would bring him back to the land of his fathers. God chose to close the divide between Heaven and earth and took it upon Himself to reach out directly to Jacob.

Thankfully, God has done the same for us. He has done this by sending His son, Jesus Christ—our first and foremost "escape route"—and also by providing the tools we need to stay on the straight and narrow once we accept Jesus as our Savior. To help us out, God has written down all the escape strategies we could ever need, all contained within the greatest emergency escape map of all—the Holy Bible.

OUR MAP

While God gave Jacob an anchor that came in the form of a dream, our anchor is the Bible. The world is like water—always moving, always changing and unsure. Without something to hold us in place, the water could easily overpower us and take us far away from where we want to be. The never-ceasing truth of God's Word is the thing holding us fast to the way He intends us to live.

But we won't stay safe and firmly grounded in the chaotic waters of the world if we don't actually *use* this anchor. What good is God's Word to us if our Bible is never opened or applied to our lives?

I know you're tired and busy—I am too. But your destiny is God's history. To understand where God wants you to be, you have to see where others have already been and how they got through. Spend time in the Word to uncover and discover God's desired path for your life. Even five minutes a day with the teachings of Christ can reorient you to where you, a child of God, need to be and how you should be living.

Some of these words and teachings are easy—presumably all of us know and agree we shouldn't kill someone or sleep with our neighbor's wife. But what about things that are less clear, like greed? Listening to the opinions of man over the voice of God? Giving (or not) to those in need? Honoring your spouse? Teaching your children to honor those in authority?

Truth be told, these things aren't as unclear as we like to make them out to be. The Bible answers most of these questions pretty easily, but you won't find the answers to these things if you don't take time to search. They are answers that you might need to dive into the Word to remember or find out. Once found, they can help you hold firm to your principles and the righteous path.

It's amazing how reorienting and rejuvenating the teachings of Christ can be. It's also true that sometimes they are not rejuvenating at all—sometimes we don't like the answers we find. But just like it's dangerous to be at sea without an anchor, so too is it dangerous to go through life without the guidance of the one who can protect you. Those pulled out to sea don't always make it back to land again. Is it worth that risk?

Reorient and rejuvenate yourself. Take at least five minutes each day to grab hold of the anchor of your faith. Dust it off, grab a highlighter, and start reading. Before you know it, five minutes will become ten, and soon you may even be setting your alarm to get up early and firmly ground yourself in God's Word.

REORGANIZE YOUR THINKING

Has anyone ever told you not to think about something? What's the first thing you do? You think about it. Telling yourself to stop won't eliminate the problem—you need a mind shift. This is no easy task, and there is no quick fix or formula we can concoct to avoid this process. However there is a solution, and it's found by applying the Word of God. Our mind must be changed (shifted) from the patterns of the world to operating daily with the mind of Christ. Philippians 2:5 says, *"Let this mind be in you, which was also in Christ Jesus."* What we continue to think about and dwell on forms into convictions of our heart, and the convictions of the heart translate into actions. Therefore, we must first shift our minds daily by applying the mind of Christ through God's Word.

The eye originally views images upside-down, but our minds reinterpret this input to allow us to see things the correct way up. The same thing goes when we apply the mind of Christ to every situation. When things get twisted and situations start to flip downward, we have the ability to reinterpret what we see through the mind of Christ.

For a moment consider and think about how you see things and the thought process that normally follows. Most people's thought processes tend to be one or more of the following categories:

1. **Unrealistic expectations:** This thought pattern occurs when the expectations you give yourself and others around you are far too high. You use words like *should* and *wish*. For example, "I should be better by now." "I wish they would just know what's bothering me." "They should know me by now." Every time we use these words in this type of context, they are associated with expectations that cannot be met, especially when we look to others or even ourselves to meet these expectations.

2. **Worst-case scenario:** This way of thinking takes something simple and blows it up into a world-ending event. For example, you wake up with a minor cough. Your mind immediately goes to the worst-case scenario of everything it could be. You find yourself researching your symptoms on Google for hours while your mind races back and forth telling you, "You're going to die." In reality, you were only experiencing some congestion in your chest.

3. **Blamer:** This occurs when we refuse to take responsibility for our thoughts and our actions. We are always avoiding the thought that at some point and time throughout the day we may be wrong, instead preferring to

deflect the blame to something or someone else.

4. **Plain and simple:** Often known as thinking in terms of "all or nothing"—things are either really good or really bad. There is no in-between. This is a dangerous thought pattern because it disables your ability to see from any viewpoint other than your own and isolates you from seeing all sides of the situation.

5. **Over-analyzer:** This thought pattern paralyzes you from making any decisions. Often known as *analysis paralysis*, it's always looking for a sure-shot solution up front. Decisions are treated as a task too complicated to follow through on and complete. In sports they consider this thought process to be "choking" or folding under pressure. Ring a bell?

6. **Reason driven by emotion:** This mentality drives you to believe that what you're feeling is fact. For instance, say you make the mistake of losing your cool and allowing your temper to get the best of you. Reason by emotion would have you believe that you're a terrible person based off of that one event. Truth is, what you're feeling is not fact, and our feelings can change in a matter of seconds if we can identify the thoughts that led us to believe these things in the first place.

Which one of these patterns would you say is relatable to what goes on in your head on a day-to-day basis?

The good news is this: we can abandon those thoughts and swap out our mind by receiving and applying the mind that God has provided for us through Christ.

THE POWER OF PRAYER

Take some time—the more the better—to pray. For all his faults and the long and winding road he took to end up at God's feet, Jacob did not often forget to pray, and sometimes he heard God answer him clearly, directing the path he should take. Prayer is a powerful tool, and one we can all use. If you aren't sure where to begin, that's okay. God's Word is packed with wisdom on the topic of prayer. I've taken the time to list a few that stick out to me that I believe you will find to be great starting points.

1. Seek the presence of God with a grateful heart. This is found in Matthew 6:9 in the line, "Our Father which art in heaven, hallowed be thy name." *Hallowed* means to make holy, pure. This salutation gives God the glory He is due, which is the best way to enter into your daily talks with Him—not with requests and a to-do list, but with praise and reverence. Start here.

2. Seek God's priorities over your own. Jesus made clear in the line, "Your kingdom come. Your will be done on earth as it is in heaven" (Matthew 6:10 NKJV), that we are to do

exactly what we've spent the last several chapters talking about—abandoning our ways, wants, and desires, and seeking instead the ways, wants, and desires of Christ. Later in Matthew we find these words: "But seek first the kingdom of God and His righteousness, and all these things shall be added to you" (NKJV). If you seek, you will find.

3. Seek the Lord's provisions to supply your daily needs. Matthew 6:11 makes this one pretty clear: "Give us this day our daily bread." God *wants* to provide for us, truly He does. Philippians 4:19 states, "But my God shall supply all your need according to his riches in glory by Christ Jesus." How sweet that is! The richness of grace, the daily provision of bread. Seek with the realization that He not only *wants* but *desires* the meet our needs.

4. Seek God's pardon for your sins and open your heart to forgiving others. This is an important one. "Forgive us our sins, just as we have forgiven those who have sinned against us" (Matthew 6:12 TLB). First John 1:9 states that if we confess our sins, He is faithful and just and will forgive us our sins and purify us from evil. Praise God! For all the low-down, dirty, rotten ways we act, God will forgive us. Amazing. God wants us to open our hearts to providing that same spirit of forgiveness to

others. Oftentimes, the anger and hatred we hold against another doesn't do a single thing to hurt the person we feel it against. Instead, it festers inside our soul and hurts *us*, the unforgiving. God knows this, and knows we need release from that unrighteous and self-inflicted pain. We are never in a place where God's forgiveness can't reach us, so long as we truly seek forgiveness.

5.   Seek God's wisdom to overcome temptation. "And lead us not into temptation, but deliver us from evil" (Matthew 6:13). In planning your escape route, keep these lines in mind: "No temptation has overtaken you except such as is common to man; but God is faithful, who will not allow you to be tempted beyond what you are able, but with the temptation will also make the way of escape, that you may be able to bear it" (1 Corinthians 10:13 NKJV). Perhaps I should have just deleted this whole chapter and let that one verse stand alone. It is simply packed with power. We see in it that temptations are *common*. God has been there and has defeated the very temptation you are being faced with.

GET PLANTED

For as the body is one, and hath many members, and all the members of that one body, being many, *are one body: so also is Christ. For by one Spirit are we all baptized into one body, whether we be Jews or Gentiles, whether we be bond or free, and have been all made to drink into one Spirit. **For the body is not one member, but many*** (1 Corinthians 12:12-14).

Part of avoiding temptation is having someone who can hold you accountable. Just as important is having a wider circle of people who can provide you with friendship and a spirit of community that embodies the teachings of Christ and the righteous lifestyle you're looking for.

After Jacob became Israel, he dedicated his life, his family, and all his land to God and God's glory. Jacob didn't just give *himself* to God, but instead he gave everyone and everything under his roof to God. He destroyed idols and wouldn't allow them. He knew that he needed all those around him to be worshipful of the one true God, thus allowing them all to worship and serve together.

With whom do you worship and serve? Do you have a church you call home? If not, then it's time you found one! I know, lots of people say they are Christian, but "church" and "the church thing" just aren't for them. But God did not make us to worship alone. There are many reasons for this, but the reasons we are talking about now have to do with influence, accountability, and community.

Influence

First Corinthians 15:33 tells us that "bad company corrupts good character" (NIV). The wiser we get in life, the more we realize the truth and importance of this sentiment. For those of you who are parents, you know you want your kids to have "good" friends. Friends whose parents you like, who get decent grades, maybe play a sport or two, and don't spend too much time in the principal's office. For those of you without kids, you probably remember your own parents worrying about this with you. Just because we are grown up and perhaps living on our own now doesn't make this any different.

This isn't to say that people who go into a brick building called a "church" every Sunday are without fault—of course they aren't. But, for good or for bad, there's a lot to be said for the power of assembling together. And when all those natural-born sinners convene on Sunday morning or mid-week service seeking Jesus, something supernatural happens.

When your spend time with these people and establish friendships with them and begin to hang out with them even outside of church walls, this same principle applies. There's nothing fake or contrived about this. It's the natural order of our world—we want to be liked, accepted, and understood, and this leads to both following along with others as well as sharing your own personality traits with others for them to follow along with you. All the better if you are pulling one another up, not pushing each other down.

That's where accountability comes in.

Accountability

Do you have an accountability group or partner? Have you heard of such a thing? If the answer is no to either question, may I suggest to you that you look into joining or starting an accountability group?

An accountability group is a small group of close friends whom you trust and who will help you stay pure and faithful as well as help you overcome sin and avoid temptation. James 5:16 states, "Therefore confess your sins to each other and pray for each other so that you may be healed. The prayer of a righteous person is powerful and effective" (NIV). This is the essential point of an accountability group that doesn't have anything to do with numbers or math.

Although we're used to hearing about peer pressure in a negative way, it really can be a positive thing as well. When you put a group of Christian, faith-minded people together in a group, they can each help one another both identify and abandon their stumbling blocks and submit to God's will. The group members lift one another up and encourage one another to grow and mature in their Christian faith.

Growth and maturity, as well as the peer pressure effect, can build up a wall of protection around you and any activities that are tempting you. When temptation crops up, you can pick up the phone or send an email or go out for coffee with the friend and tell him or her what's happening in your life. They can help talk you out of bad decision-making, pray for you, or give you strength to say no to whatever it is that's beckoning to you.

An added benefit to an accountability group is that you will undoubtedly build even closer friendships with the members of your group, which, in turn, strengthens your Christian support community.

Community

I've been using the word "community" a lot, but what exactly is it? One definition is "a feeling of fellowship with others, as a result of sharing common attitudes, interests, and goals." Certainly that is a textbook definition, but trust me, when I say "community" I mean something much deeper than that.

Community means that you're a part of a local body all moving in the same direction.

Jacob was able to build his own godly community by committing all he had—including all the many people living under his roof and on his land—to God, but in today's world building community is outrageously hard. There are innumerable books, blogs, sermons, and how-to series about how to build community once you're an adult. People are busy! They have jobs, kids, spouses, and struggles that keep them from spending time getting to know people on a level deep enough to sustain a true, long-lasting friendship. But it is possible!

Part of your exit strategy for when temptation strikes has got to be having a community of believers to support you and hold you accountable. We give in to temptation in our moments of weakness. Affairs can happen after a fight with a spouse—having friends to call on who are committed to reconciling your marriage will give you the support you need. We lash out at our kids when we're stressed by the demands of life—a community of like-minded folks want you to succeed in raising godly children and will provide respite when you've reached the end of your rope.

I could continue with this list for a long time but I won't. I think the point has been made—when planning your exit strategies, be sure to include surrounding yourself with believing friends who will support you, love you, and hold you accountable for your thoughts and actions.

KNOW YOUR MISSION

Your escape route won't do you much good if you can't locate yourself on the emergency map—that's why the little star, "you are here," is on there. Maps can be confusing and hard to read, with lines and arrows shooting off in all directions, pointing this way and that. By locating the star, you can make a logical and informed decision about which line and arrow will point you toward safety.

When you're building your spiritual escape route, do you know where it is that you're standing?

God has gifted us and called us all in one form or another. In 1 Peter 4:10 we read, "Each of you should use whatever gift you have received to serve others, as faithful stewards of God's grace in its various forms" (NIV). Another way to think of a "gift" or "calling" is as a mission. A mission is an operation or assignment given to you by a higher authority. W. Clement Stone said, "When you discover your mission, you will feel its demand. It will fill you with enthusiasm and a burning desire to get to work on it." Acts 20:24 states, "I only want to complete my mission and finish the work that the Lord Jesus gave me to do, which is to declare the Good News about the grace of God" (GNT).

Well, that's great, right? You're supposed to do this most important thing, assigned by none other than Jesus Himself, and odds are good you have absolutely no idea what that mission is. So how do you discover it?

In part, you go back and reread Phase One of this book. You have to understand that it's only in *abandoning* yourself fully to God, submitting heart and soul to His will and *only* His will, that you will find your calling, your fulfillment, and be the righteous child of God He wants you to be.

And sometimes, as was the case with Jacob, God is telling us all along what our mission is, and we simply don't listen. Or, we only listen to what we want to hear. Ask yourself: Where do your talents lie? What do people tell you over and over you're good at? What makes you feel fulfilled? What breaks your heart? What makes you cry tears of joy? Pray on these questions and then *listen*. Don't jump on every mission trip, volunteer activity, and non-profit board you encounter. Just…be still. Wait until you feel God's tug on your heart. Oftentimes, we need to look back over the trajectory of life and see where our path has been straight and narrow, full of goodness and ease, and where it has been twisted and rocky, full of bumps and heartache. What were you doing during the good times? During the bad?

God probably isn't going to speak directly to us or come to us so clearly in a dream. More likely than not, God is going to show you your path by granting you ease in those moments during which you are exercising your gifting, and stress and grief when you are not. He's given you all the clues, but you're going to have to snoop them out for yourself. Or, you could ask some of the people God has blessed you with—those in your church community. Have others pray for and with you, maybe even seek out a meeting or two with the pastor. There are even online tests for figuring out your areas of God-given strength!

If you know your gift(s), you are that much more likely to find your mission. Your mission will firmly root you in the place you want and are supposed to be and set you on a trajectory of God-willed success, making it all the easier to avoid temptation when it comes knocking.

PUTTING IT ALL TOGETHER

Hopefully you're ready now to move forward with your two-prong plan of attack of shunning and planning: Shun those places, people, and things that dig deep into your weak areas, and draw up a detailed plan of your escape route. Somewhere in there factor in building a life and strategy that take into consideration your calling so that you can pursue your mission, that greatest of gifts from God.

For prayer and reflection:

- What is your escape route?

- If you don't have one, how can you put one in place? Which of the previously mentioned action steps can you put into place in your own life?

- What might your mission be? How can you go about finding it? Ask those who truly know and love you, and whom you trust, to tell you what comes to their hearts for you.

"God has given us the tools we need to get out of any tempting situation we may be faced with."

#ABANDON

Chapter Five

ABANDON YOUR OUTLOOK

How do you view life? How do you see yourself, and what do you perceive as your role and worth to society? The answers to those questions play a tremendous part in the quality of living you experience. We tend to accept one of four major evaluations for our life—the way we see ourselves, the way others see us, the way the enemy sees us, and the way God sees us.

A negative mind will never produce a positive life, and a positive outlook will position you to see what God sees. But if you are like most people, there is no one tougher on you than *you*. You will quickly discover that discerning and living out God's plan for your life is almost impossible when you magnify every fault, every problem, every imperfection that you (think you) possess. It isn't possible to live fully in your God-given ability when you feel damaged by life itself as well as the sinful thoughts and actions you may struggle with. And it's certainly impossible to live the good life as a child of God when you sit around wondering how God could ever love and use someone as broken and damaged as you.

A negative mind will never produce a positive life, and a positive outlook will position you to see what God sees.

#ABANDON

If we only highlight our flaws, it will certainly be tough at times to feel like a beloved child of God. No one knows as well as you do the wrong you have not only done, but have thought in life. The same applies to what goes on in your head and mind on a daily basis—no one knows but you. Sometimes, it's how others have treated us that keeps us from feeling like God's beloved and enjoying our blessings. Maybe you've been mistreated, abused, repeatedly told you are not good enough.

The truth is, every single one of us has been damaged in some way, whether by our own mistakes or the mistakes others have made toward us. More likely than not, it's a combination of the two. Regardless, God loves you, wants you, and can use you, no matter what condition or state you are in.

DAMAGED GOODS

No matter what condition you are in—broken, damaged, or in shambles—God still wants you. Even better, He is able to make you whole again. Through Jesus Christ, God has made us a guarantee that He will restore us and transform us into something far greater than we could ever imagine.

As we've already discussed, there are times we may think the restoration will never come, but the author of Psalms tells us it is well worth the wait: "I wait for the Lord, my soul waits...with the Lord there is mercy, and with Him is abundant redemption" (Psalms 130:6-7 NKJV).

There is no saint or sinner greater or less in the eyes of God. Jesus is the great equalizer—He came to save all who would receive Him. And included in that "all," believe it or not, is *you*. Jacob was, of course, before Jesus's time. But God's desire to accept us all, saint or sinner, is evident in Jacob's story.

God saw and knew Jacob's full potential. He saw that beneath the lies and deceit lay a prince, and so God repaired Jacob's brokenness and made him whole again.

MADE WHOLE THROUGH BROKENNESS

God will take us just as we are, brokenness and all. In fact, our brokenness serves the purpose of bringing us closer to God and enabling us to see what He sees. In brokenness we learn righteousness as we feel the very real impact of the ways of mercy instead of judgment in our lives. Does your heart break for what God's does? Can you see through His eyes? When that happens, you can't help but be changed in all that you do. No way you can see with God's eyes and live a life apart from Him.

We can see how Jacob's brokenness caused him to pursue God, and how God was there for Jacob in his time of need. In his greatest time of fear, Jacob prayed: "O God of my father Abraham and God of my father Isaac, the Lord who said to me, 'Return to your country and to your family, and I will deal well with you': I am not worthy of the least of all the mercies and of all the truth which You have shown Your servant" (Genesis 32:9-10 NKJV).

Jacob feared repercussions for the deceitful actions he had taken against Esau. In so feeling, Jacob was acknowledging that what he had done to Esau was wrong—that Jacob had committed a harmful act born of his broken nature. Jacob saw himself clearly, and went to God asking for mercy and grace (although lacking in trust that God would fulfill earlier promises to Jacob). In this we see how brokenness brought Jacob closer to God when he realized his desperation for protection. Jacob's petition to God was the opposite of his typical mindset that he could handle things on his own, knew what should be done, and that God wasn't necessary. His brokenness caused him to shun his independence and walk toward God, who, of course, did protect him and accept him just as he was. By the time Jacob returned home, he had become fully changed. No longer did he lie and deceive. Instead he gave his all to following and worshiping the Lord.

> Unmerited favor doesn't mean that we simply do what we want to do and it's all good.
>
> #ABANDON

We know that Jesus brought grace—unmerited favor—to us through His death on the cross. No longer do we have to work our way to salvation or God's good graces. *Unmerited favor, however, doesn't mean that we simply do what we want to do and it's all good.* Instead, when we receive God's grace, commend our lives to Christ, and are filled with the joy of His love, a heart transformation should occur within us. Remember, the "heart" is our mind, our will, and our soul—all dwelling places for the Holly Spirit. When the Holy Spirit has taken up residence in your heart, it crowds out the bad and the ugly and expands the good, driving us closer and closer to God not because we *have* to draw closer to Him, but because we *want* to.

Think of it this way:

As I mentioned before, there was a time in my life right before my father's death when I walked away from the lifestyle I should have been living. Wrong seemed to be right, and the right way to live didn't seem to be the thing for me anymore. My circle of friends and influencers changed from people encouraging me to stay focused to people encouraging me to focus on making money by any means necessary. None of which were good or legal for that matter. Somewhere in all of this, I lost sight of who I was. When I looked in the mirror, most of the time I couldn't even recognize who was staring back at me. I'm sure my parents felt the same way at some point or another, undoubtedly asking themselves, "Who *is* this person occupying my son's body?"

As much as my choice of lifestyle disappointed them, they continued to love me and pray for me. They understood that the seeds that they planted in my life, at some point and some time, were going to reproduce a harvest. Unbeknownst to me, just as with plants and flowers, I had two types of seed at work on the inside of me. The poor choices and sinful lifestyle I opted to live only lasted for a season—better known in botany as an *annual seed*. In comparison, the seeds of love and faith my parents sowed and planted were *perennial*; meaning the seeds they sowed had the strength to survive, flourishing and blossoming time and time again. A parent's love can weather even the toughest of times.

Parents put up with sleepless nights when their children are infants, deal with tantrums from their toddlers, and muddle miserably through all sorts of craziness during the teenage years. Through all this, parents are supposed to love the child who is exhausting them, frustrating them, and pushing them to their very limits. Supposedly, in return for the parents' love, a child will, once grown, act in accord with his or her parents' upbringing and wishes. We see this hope reflected in Proverbs 22:6, in which it is written: "Train up a child in the way he should go: and when he is old, he will not depart from it."

But as children begin to separate from their parents, a pretty standard progression tends to occur—the child rebels against the parents' unconditional love but then, eventually, blossoms and flourishes under the parents' care and begins to act with respect. Not because the parents *force* the child to, but because out of true love for his or her parents the child *truly feels* respect and a desire to please the ones who have been so accepting of all the child's faults.

We may not want to admit it, but this is exactly how we treat our relationship with Jesus. Not in every instance, of course, but there does tend to be a pretty standard progression. When we first accept Jesus, we are like infants. We depend on Jesus for everything and don't want to ever be separated from the one we so love and adore. Time passes, life wears on us, bad things happen, and our fervor for Jesus lessens. We get mad and ask questions like, "Why, God? Why haven't You answered my prayer? Saved my husband? Healed my child?" And we throw tantrums at the injustice of it all. After a while, these tantrums turn into the faith-based version of sneaking out at night—we think we no longer need to follow the rules established by the one who previously kept us so enthralled as brand new Christians, being led by the Spirit of God. We tire of the rules, and so we begin to break or bend them. *We assert our independence, and God's Word begins to lose its prominence.* Note that this can happen even when we're faithfully attending church and putting on the day-to-day appearance of living the Christian life. Our hearts can be rebellious even when our actions are not.

After a few months or years of paying our own bills, cooking our own food, and cleaning up our own messes, we realize how hard being without Christ is, and that Jesus only wanted what was best for us all along. The best-case scenario ending is that we mature and come back to Christ, asking Him how we should live to make it day by day. In our walk with Christ, this means that the knowledge of

His everlasting grace gives us a heartfelt and true desire to serve Him and follow His teachings by living a life of righteousness.

Some of us don't follow this pattern, of course. But what is universally true is that a full realization of God's unconditional and whole-hearted love should bring about in us a true desire to live a life that pleases Him. The point of grace isn't to become comfortable and complacent in our spiritual life, reassuring ourselves that it will all be okay because of God's love and mercy. That attitude will never challenge us to become more like Christ, to see what He sees and walk like He walks. It will never challenge us to abandon our old, unholy, and junk-filled ways.

In Ephesians 2:8-9 we read, "For by grace are ye saved through faith; and that not of yourselves: it is the gift of God: not of works." But we also read in 1 John 3:7-9:

> *Dear children, do not let anyone lead you astray. The one who does what is right is righteous, just as he is righteous. The one who does what is sinful is of the devil, because the devil has been sinning from the beginning. The reason the Son of God appeared was to destroy the devil's work.* ***No one who is born of God will continue to sin, because God's seed remains in them; they cannot go on sinning, because they have been born of God*** *(NIV).*

In Romans 12:2, we see the desire put this way: "And be not conformed to this world: but be ye transformed by the renewing of your mind, and ye may prove what is that good, and acceptable, and perfect, will of God." We are infused with a desire to transform ourselves into people more like Jesus.

Now, there are all kinds of theological discussions we could get into here, but the point, when you get right down to it, is that a life led by the Spirit of God will always lead you toward righteousness. We see this happen to Jacob upon his return home, when he gives himself, his land, and all the people in his household over to God.

For thought:

- Do you believe God can make or remake you into something remarkable?

- How have you experienced your own brokenness bringing you closer to God?

- Do you try to see what He sees?

*"In brokenness we learn righteousness
as we feel the very real impact
of the ways of mercy instead
of judgment in our lives."*

#ABANDON

Phase Three

THE CHANGE

In Phase One of this book we faced a choice: will we abandon our lives to God, giving ourselves over to a life of continual obedience, purpose, and living fulfilled? Or will we continue to hold on too tight to the things *we* want for our lives and follow selfish and shallow ways?

In Phase Two we addressed the daily challenges we'll face once we make the decision to live a life for the Lord.

Now, in this last section, we'll focus on the change that will and must take place inside of us so that we can begin to see God's desired manifestations around us. We must learn how to control our feelings, emotions, and moods such that we are living, breathing examples of the goodness of God in our daily lives. Our mind must be completely made new. We must see the blessings within a trial and learn how to find joy even in the midst of pain. Our hearts, minds, and souls must close themselves to negativity and open themselves to the positive and glorious abundance that comes from being a beloved child of God. We'll focus on those times when walking the walk becomes a struggle because of trials encountered during certain seasons of life. In those times, it's important to think back to the awesome things God has already done in your life.

We'll also talk about how God's unconditional acceptance and the radical grace of Jesus Christ will change our life of complacency to a life lived outrageously. Never be compliant with complacency. Instead, be persistent in your pursuit to experience the radical love and grace of Christ! The habit of persistence yields the reward of victory.

Chapter Six

SHOULDA, WOULDA, COULDA

How many times in life have you thought, "Shoulda, woulda, coulda?" Shoulda done better, woulda only if, if things had been different I coulda. Of course, none of these actually change the past or provide valid solutions to whatever might be at hand. All these kinds of thoughts do is bury us deeper in self-doubt, regret, and defeatism.

What we wouldn't give for just one little do-over, right? Anything to stop the replays from repeating over and over again in our head as we try our best to think of the perfect response to whatever situation we were facing at that time in the past. But those are the three key words we should focus on—*in the past.*

INDIANA JONES AND THE LAND OF REGRET

Have you ever done or been a part of something that you later regretted? I have. Believe it or not there was a time in my life long, long ago (wink, wink) when my role model for everything pertaining to all things was Indiana Jones. I wanted to be and look like him in every way; I had the hat, pants, tan shirt, boots, and even the leather jacket. The only thing I was missing was the infamous Indiana Jones whip. My parents—being the awesome parents that they were—knew just how much I loved this fictional character, and so they bought me a whip to complete my look…and attached to it a long list of instructions of the things I was not allowed to do with it. One of those instructions was, "Do not lasso the whip around any trees or branches."

Well, I'm pretty sure you know how this story goes. I was completely obedient and did what they told me to do, right? Wrong. As soon as they left the house, I scouted the perfect tree branch to lasso my whip around. After three minutes of searching high and low, I found it! I looked around a couple of times to make sure nobody was looking, and after I was assured of that, I got on top of a pile of fire wood and began to twirl the whip around my head like a cow wrangler. After some intense twirling, I latched the whip onto a branch, gave it a tug to make sure it was secure, and began my adventurist descent. What I didn't take notice of was the four-by-four on the ground with a nail sticking out of the top. By the time I saw the nail it was too late—there was nothing I could do to avoid it. I was able to land one foot on the ground, but the other wasn't as fortunate. My right foot landed right on the nail; the force of the impact drove the nail all the way through my shoe and out the top of my foot.

Staying fairly cool considering the circumstance, I tried to remove the nail and board before anybody caught wind of what was going on. I pulled and tugged to no avail. Finally I gave up. I had to regretfully (and painfully) go in the house with a long four-by-four nailed to my foot and patiently wait for my parents to get back home.

Some time later my parents arrived and saw me sitting on the couch. They didn't have to ask what happened; they immediately knew by the look on my face. My dad sat down without saying a word, lifted my leg and the board attached to it, and pulled my foot loose. He then began the cleaning process by pouring rubbing alcohol right into the open hole on the top of my foot. The pain was severe, but it wasn't nearly as painful as regretfully looking my parents in the face, longing for their forgiveness.

Like this incident, some of our past decisions have led us down the road of regret, and on this journey you may find pit stops called embarrassment, disappointment, and shame. But the good news is this: your story doesn't have to end with pain and regret. Your heavenly Father longs to forgive you, erase the regret, clean you, and give you a fresh start.

We can't enjoy the victories of today if we're continually dwelling on the defeats of yesterday. To leave the land of regret firmly where it belongs—behind us—it's important to remember that our goal moving forward is not to strive to be perfect. When we strive to be perfect we are relying on our own strength and not God's. Abandoning the journey of perfectionism frees us of defeat and allows us to experience victory through the grace of Jesus. If we rely on our own strength seeking to be perfected we will fail. God's

Word tells us that He has redeemed us and that we shall not be overwhelmed (see Isaiah 43:1-2). In fact, we can't enjoy much of anything when we're too caught up in the miseries of looking back, wishing we could have been nicer, stronger, smarter, prettier, healthier, wiser—whatever the "shoulda, woulda, coulda" may be. To be sure, sometimes looking back is a good thing. We can examine the areas of life where we made mistakes and try to figure out what we could do better in the future to avoid those mistakes. Whatever situation arose before may very well happen again, and with a little self-examination and soul searching that regretful moment from the past may serve us well in succeeding in the future.

> We can't enjoy the victories of today if we're continually dwelling on the defeats of yesterday.
> #ABANDON

Another *must* for keeping life on a forward trajectory is *forgiveness*. God already knows what you did in the past that has you so upset. He saw it when you made the mistake, and He sees you now in your regret. And you know what? He's never once been surprised by the things you've done, because, as He tells us: "I know what I'm doing. I have it all planned out—plans to take care of you, not abandon you, plans to give you the future you hope for" (Jeremiah 29:11 MSG). This tells us that God knows our deepest feeling-s and sees our regret more than anyone else can. God knows what our tomorrows hold, and if we turn to Him He will guide us forward in reaching those tomorrows. We must hand our worries over to Him in faithfulness, knowing He sees all, guides all, and loves all.

Sometimes the regrets we need to turn over aren't simply the fruits of past mistakes or embarrassing moments. Sometimes they are much deeper than that—the harvest from past sins.

The pleasure of sin is quickly replaced by shame, regret, and feeling distanced from God. You know when you don't return an email or phone call for a while, and eventually you feel like you just *can't* return the email or call because you've waited such an embarrassingly long time and there's no good excuse? That's what our sins and regrets cause us to do with God sometimes. We are ashamed to face Him, and so we pull away. And the more we pull away, the more distant we feel. And finally it feels like we can just never return. How could we explain why we were gone so long?

But you know what? God already knows everything that there is to know about you. He saw the sin. He feels your regret. He sees you pull away in your shame. And He knows whether or not you'll come back. And when you do, He will hear your confession and embrace you with arms stretched wide.

He isn't going to lecture you or punish you. He is simply going to…accept you. Bless you. Forgive you. Jesus has washed it all away.

This should give you all the strength necessary to find self-forgiveness for past mistakes and live fully and joyfully in today's victories. There is nothing you can do that will surprise God, and no amount of regret or shame is too much for Him to help you overcome. He will use your life to display the powers of His amazing grace.

I'M GOING THROUGH

We can get caught up in *seasons* of regretful actions, not just mere moments. There may be an entire decade or more of life you lived in ways that shame you now and fill your heart with regret. Both living in these times as well as reflecting regretfully on them can bring us down into darkness—dark mood, thoughts, feelings.

When these times come, it will be helpful to remember that they will pass and you will heal. Valleys are the places we walk through to get to the mountain top, not places where we dwell eternally. In 1 Peter we read that "There is wonderful joy ahead, even though the going is rough for a while down here" (1 Peter 1:6 TLB). Peter further tells us that life isn't just going to be an easy stroll; it's going to have lows and tough times, but he also reminds us that there is wonderful joy ahead. Our life's victory comes through Christ, and we are promised an eternity—*an eternity*—full of peace, joy, happiness, and fulfillment. Our valleys are temporary, and there is an eternity of glory that overrides them all.

Often there are lessons to be learned even in the lowest of moments. We need to take those lessons and move on, not dwell in shame, regret, and embarrassment for all those shoulda, woulda, couldas. To move out of that mentality you must:

1. Value Christ above all things. He is worth abandoning it all for.

2. Trust that Christ will provide for your every need.

3. Pursue Christ above all.

4. Advance at all costs. Make whatever changes you must to be spiritually healthy.

"Abandoning the journey of perfectionism frees us of defeat and allows us to experience victory through the grace of Jesus."

#ABANDON

Chapter Seven

WHO AM I—TODAY?

SWEET AND SOUR

Have you ever paid attention to how quickly our feelings—and oftentimes the feelings of those around us—can fluctuate so quickly and frequently throughout the day? Maybe we wake up happy, but within minutes of dealing with the hustle and bustle of the morning routine things take a turn for the worst. Even more extreme is that some days we feel on top of everything, like we can conquer the world and everything in it, and on others we feel stressed or at our lowest of lows, wondering how we'll ever manage to make it through even one more day.

These extreme ups and downs are fairly normal and are so commonplace (although, as we'll come to see, not unavoidable) that they have been written about in literature for centuries—think Dr. Jekyll and Mr. Hyde—as well as alluded to in the Bible.

Interestingly enough, Jacob is at times referred to in the Bible as "Jacob" and other times referred to as "Israel." The reason for this within the book of Genesis is to show us how Jacob grew and changed in his faith, but in other areas of the Bible the reason for alternating between names isn't as clear. In fact, in Numbers, we see both "Jacob" and "Israel" used within the same sentence: "Surely there is no enchantment against Jacob, neither is there any divination against Israel: according to this time it shall be said of Jacob and of Israel, What hath God wrought!" (Numbers 23:23).

The two different names of Jacob are used here because of the two underlying personality types we've come to associate with Jacob and his progression from deceiver to prince. The word *enchantment* is tied to "Jacob," and *divination* is tied to "Israel." *Enchantment* is a word meaning invocation of demons, which fits with Jacob's personality of deceit, and *divination* means to discover something by means of supernatural powers, as is fitting for Israel, a prince of God.

How do others perceive you and your actions? Are you known as Jacob or as Israel? Likely a little of both, depending on what you're allowing to control your feelings on any given day or in any given moment.

The problem is, most of us don't allow *anything* to control our feelings. Whatever we feel is what we show, and we feel whatever it is that comes to us first—unbidden, without prayer, reflection, or consideration for others. That, my friend, is an attitude we must hastily abandon.

THE FUKUSHIMA REACTOR

When I see someone losing their cool—maybe a friend, a person in the checkout line, another driver on the road, whomever it may be—I can almost see the billow of smoke mushroom from their heads, and a nuclear disaster comes to mind. One of the most recent ones we can specifically relate to is the Fukushima Daiichi disaster of 2011.

The interesting thing about the Fukushima explosion is that it didn't happen of its own accord. Instead, a series of events took place. The nuclear plant was impacted by a tsunami, and the tsunami occurred because of an earthquake. The earthquake happened because two pieces of the earth's foundation shifted. And like so many things in our lives that lie under the surface unseen, if we're not careful to spiritually maintain them, before we know it one thing will lead to another, and we will subsequently find ourselves cleaning up the mess of our emotional disaster.

When we are led by the Spirit of God, it should cause us to reflect and regulate what stems from the branches of our emotions.

#ABANDON

Think of it: A colleague at work gets into an argument with his spouse before coming to work (the earthquake). He gets to work still frustrated over what happened earlier and yells at his assistant (the tsunami). His assistant then flies off the handle and becomes an angry ball of fury, taking his anger out on all those he encounters that day—the clerk at the dry cleaner's, the cable guy, his kids, etc. The anger spreads and mushrooms in a nuclear reaction to one person's bad day and inability to control his feelings, until finally the colleague sees that far too many have felt the sting of what could have been very different, had he been able to better handle a difficult moment. I'm sure at some point and time you've experienced this domino effect. Maybe you've even tried to stop it. But it's hard, once those dominos start to fall. The best thing we can possibly do in this instance is allow God to illuminate and address the unseen. When we are led by the Spirit of God, it should cause us to reflect and regulate what stems from the branches of our emotions.

We've talked about anger, so let's focus on what stems from that branch. Did you know that "anger" (an emotion) can show itself through the feelings of:

- Irritation/annoyance

- Bitterness

- Exasperation

- Envy

We think of the items on the above list as things *separate* from anger—different things altogether. But that isn't so—instead, they are all branches of the same tree. Now it's time to do a little pruning. Here's the same list again, with a corresponding equal and opposite reaction you could choose instead:

- Irritation/annoyance—calm, relaxed

- Bitterness—accepting, grateful

- Exasperation—understanding, patient

- Envy—confident, complete

Replacing one with the other is, of course, easy to say but tougher to do.

EMOTIONS VERSUS FEELINGS VERSUS MOOD: CONTROLLING THEM ALL

You may be surprised to learn that feelings, emotions, and mood are not the same thing. Surprised? It's true, and understanding the difference between the three can make all the difference when it comes to following God, as well as the blueprint He has set before us to abandon our ways for His.

Emotions

Emotions are brought on by a person, situation, or object. Emotions are important because they give importance to things beyond ourselves. A song may cause us to feel a strong reaction of nostalgia. That same song may cause someone else to feel sadness. Both of these are emotions brought up by a subjective thing (a song) that exists outside of who we are. Emotions are our individual perceptions of what's around us, and they determine from what we derive pleasure and displeasure. Emotions can protect

149

us—such as the fight or flight reaction we get when facing a dangerous situation—and are essential for survival. They are temporary, but they establish the long-lasting *feelings* that carry us through our lives.

Feelings

Feelings are born of emotions. When emotions—natural, inherent, unbidden—stick around long enough, they give birth in our psyches to *feelings*. Meaning, our emotions teach us how we feel about certain things. Our natural, reflexive emotion upon seeing a newborn baby is joy. That emotion of joy leads to happiness, a feeling, of loving our child. The joy is fleeting; the love is sustained throughout the life of the parent and child.

Mood

If you've ever been around someone in a bad mood, you know that they may not be expressly *saying* they are in a bad mood, but every grumpy action they take demonstrates it. Same for someone in a joyful mood—they may not go around saying, "I'm so joyful!" but they may indeed go around whistling and smiling and generally lifting everyone's spirits through their pleasant *mood*.

Moods can last for quite a while, and oftentimes we don't even know what has caused the mood—angry, happy, or otherwise—just that we wake feeling a particular way.

WHAT THE BIBLE HAS TO SAY

The Bible has a lot of advice about how we should control our emotions, feelings, and moods, and that is but one more way daily reading the Word of God can keep us centered on living a godly life. Solomon wrote in Proverbs 17:27 that "The one who has knowledge uses words with restraint, and whoever has understanding is even-tempered" (NIV).

Godly Friends

You can better reach the level of knowledge and understanding to be restrained and even-tempered by following some of the same courses we've outlined before—surrounding yourself with the right kind of peers. "Blessed is the man who walks not in the counsel of the ungodly, nor stands in the path of sinners, nor sits in the seat of the scornful; but his delight is in the law of the Lord" (Psalms 1:1-2 NKJV). I'm sure you know what I mean—we have all had those friends who urge us on in our complaints. Instead of offering empathy and redirection, they offer empathy and add fire to the flames: "She shouldn't have done that! That's terrible and you should give her a piece of your mind. If I were you, I'd never speak to her again." Or, "He is such a jerk! You give him what he deserves." Whereas a godly friend would express, "She shouldn't have done that, but maybe there's a reason for it. Why don't you try to talk to her and work things out," or, "Yes, that wasn't very nice of him, but you love each other and should work toward forgiveness."

There's a very big difference in friendship here. One will cause the dominos to fall all the faster, the other may keep them (and you!) from falling apart altogether.

Think Before You Speak

We all know we should think before we speak, but we often speak off the cuff and out of reaction anyway. Solomon advises us that, "Any enterprise is built by wise planning, becomes strong through common sense, and profits wonderfully by keeping abreast of the facts" (Proverbs 24:3-4 TLB). Do you have all, or even most, of the facts? Have you thought about your words? If the answer to either or both of these questions is no, then keep wise counsel by keeping your thoughts to yourself.

Don't Just "Think," Think Long Term

Sure, you can win that fight with your friend/spouse/parent/co-worker. You know just what to say, using the right cutting words to bring that person down and declare yourself the victor. And oh how tempting it is to bring out those cutting words and hurl them at the person we're battling with in the heat of the moment. Don't do it. Winning a battle isn't as important as "winning the war," and we win the war by having sustaining, loving, caring relationships with all those around us. It may feel good in the moment to deal the crushing blow, but those actions will always come back to bite us and always do more damage to others than we can see on the surface. Save both yourself and your sparring partner the pain; proceed with love, keeping the long-term goal, not short-term gratification, in mind.

Decide Who You Want to Be

We are responsible to a great extent for how we come off to people and how they perceive us. "But wisdom is proved right by her deeds" (Matthew 11:18-19 NIV). How true this is! It is up to *you* how you respond to situations, and that will determine how you're perceived by others. The more you think about your actions and responses and work toward controlling your reactions and feelings through the help of God, the easier it will become.

Turn the Light On

This is connected to building your reputation: "Let your light so shine before men, that they may see your good works and glorify your Father in Heaven" (Matthew 5:16 NKJV). How do you let your light shine? Do you cut off people in traffic or let cars go ahead of you? Do you lose patience with your kids or try to understand things at their level? Do you get frustrated when those you supervise get things wrong, or do you patiently teach them the right way?

I can remember vividly being in the lobby of a hotel in Chicago watching guests of the hotel go in and out. If someone wanted to leave or enter the hotel, the hotel was kind enough to have positioned at the door a "door opener." If someone needed luggage removed from or placed in his or her vehicle, the doorman was there to assist. If someone needed a taxi, he was there to assist. If traffic got a little too hectic around the entry of the hotel, he was there to assist.

The interesting thing is, despite him assisting these people, very few stopped to thank him for the services he provided, and even fewer stopped to thank him monetarily (by tipping him).

Which made me wonder, how many people have opened significant doors in my life, and I have yet to thank or bless them?

So often we as individuals tend to think that our abilities got us in the door, when in all honesty it was the favor of God shown to us through the person holding the door open.

I love the way Dr. Mike Murdock, who has been a long-time family friend, explained it, "Seeds of honor can create a harvest for the future you desire. If you desire to walk through great doors, bless the person who opened the door for you."

> Make it a priority to honor those
> who open doors for you.
>
> #ABANDON

Many may think of "letting your light shine" as evangelizing through words or serving others through volunteering, and both those things are true. But letting our light shine is something we can and should do every single day in every action we take, so that others may see the glory of God within us. Make it a priority to honor those who open doors for you.

SO, JACOB OR ISRAEL—*YOU* DECIDE

Now that you understand a bit more about the often unexplainable and tumultuous rumblings that take place inside of you and have seen what the Bible says about learning to keep those rumblings in check and at bay, you are much better prepared to be the calm, Christ-illuminating person God intends for you to be.

"So often we as individuals tend to think that our abilities got us in the door, when in all honesty it was the favor of God shown to us through the person holding the door open."

#ABANDON

Chapter Eight

.

ENCORE

It's amazing how quickly we forget God's faithfulness when we are faced with new challenges. Our perspective gets fuzzy and our faith gets shaken due to the looming mountain of problems we face. When obstacles come our way, we should quickly hit the rewind button on our minds and remind ourselves of how God has been faithful to us in the past time and time again.

This is a similar situation to what we discussed earlier—following your own will. When you follow your own will and fight God's plan for your life, you are doubting God's faithfulness. One of the greatest things we could ever learn is that some things can only be learned in the storms or tough times of life. Each storm and problem has a purpose. Your faith is being strengthened by your struggle. When your situation screams *give up*…faith whispers *keep pushing*. It will all be worth it.

Remember: God is at work even when you are at the lowest moment of your life. You may be stuck, but God isn't. He knows how He's going to pull you out of the quicksand you think you're in, but you must *trust* in Him to do that.

> When obstacles come our way, we should quickly hit the rewind button on our minds and remind ourselves of how God has been faithful to us in the past time and time again.
>
> #ABANDON

You can't force the good to come, but what you can do is take control of your own actions and reactions. You could decide to be fed up with waiting for God, to be mad at life over the trials you encounter, and bitter because you don't have the "perfect" life you dream of. It's highly doubtful that this attitude will get you anywhere near where you want to be.

In Romans 5:3-4 we read the happy news, "We continue to shout our praise even when we're hemmed in with troubles, because we know how troubles can develop passionate patience in us, and how that patience in turn forges the tempered steel of virtue" (MSG). Inner peace begins the moment you choose not to allow another person, event, or circumstance to control your emotions.

This goes back to Paul's crazy admonishment to his shipmates when they are being tossed at sea. "Be of good cheer," he told them. Paul knew that being in that scary situation was one of the best ways they could all come to fully trust and rely on God. He also knew it was a true test of faith.

> Each storm and problem has a purpose. When your situation screams *give up*…faith whispers *keep pushing*. It will all be worth it.
>
> #ABANDON

God didn't give them smooth sailing. Instead, He gave every man on that boat a way to prove their trust and faithfulness in Him. God does a work in our lives by building our character and our faith. What about your character do you need to work on? What do you want to change the most about yourself? The power to change comes from God and you, working together. Your part comes down to the choices you make.

In addition to building our faith and character, God also often uses a crisis to get our attention and to position us for something far greater—good moments often become good memories while bad moments become good lessons. No matter the circumstance, God can turn your barriers into blessings.

In Genesis we read, "So Jacob was left alone, and a man wrestled with him till daybreak. When the man saw that he could not overpower him, he touched the socket of Jacob's hip so that his hip was wrenched as he wrestled with the man" (Genesis 32:24-25 NIV). A few verses later we find out that Jacob wasn't wrestling a man after all—he was wrestling God!

> Good moments often become good memories while bad moments become good lessons. No matter the circumstance, God can turn your barriers into blessings.
>
> #ABANDON

This is representative of the struggles we face. When Jacob encountered God there on the banks of the Jabbok River, Jacob was fleeing Laban and about to encounter Esau, who was out to extract revenge on Jacob. Jacob was overcome with the burdens he faced, and he was tired of running. That night, when Jacob wrestled God, God struck Jacob with a crippling blow: Jacob would forever limp from the damage God did to his hip. But at the end of the struggle we read that God blessed him there (see Genesis 32:29). Struggle though we might, it is only through reconciliation with God and His great plan for us that we can be blessed.

We also see in this wrestling match that God forced Jacob to declare his name. "What's your name?" God asked. "Jacob," Jacob replied. In this moment, Jacob admits his faults to God. Because *Jacob* means independent from God and deceiver, Jacob is admitting to none other than God his selfishness and deceit. Once Jacob confesses this, he is well on his way to becoming a changed man.

When Jacob took the active role of admitting his sins to God, God was then able to do a good work in Jacob. As you can see, change isn't up to God alone. We have to play an active part, and the best way to know how the script reads is to open up God's Word.

LETTING GOD RENAME YOU

It took Jacob a while to learn this lesson. In fact, God had to twice rename him before Jacob got the point!

The first renaming happens in Genesis 32:

> *Then he said, "Let me go, for the dawn is break-*
> *ing." But he said, "I will not let you go unless*
> *you bless me." So he said to him, "What is your*
> *name?" And he said, "Jacob."*
>
> *He said, "Your name shall no longer be Jacob, but*
> *Israel; for you have striven with God and with*
> *men and have prevailed." Then Jacob asked him*
> *and said, "Please tell me your name." But he said,*
> *"Why is it that you ask my name?" And he blessed*
> *him there* (Genesis 32:26-29 NASB).

And the second is in Genesis 35:

> *Then God appeared to Jacob again when he came*
> *from Paddan-aram, and He blessed him. God said*
> *to him, "Your name is Jacob; you shall no longer*
> *be called Jacob, but Israel shall be your name."*
> *Thus He called him Israel. God also said to him,*
> *"I am God Almighty; be fruitful and multiply;*

a nation and a company of nations shall come
from you, and kings shall come forth from you.
The land which I gave to Abraham and Isaac, I
will give it to you, and I will give the land to your
descendants after you" (Genesis 35:9-12 NASB).

Why did Jacob have to be renamed two different times? Jacob called continually for blessings, yet even when they were given Jacob seemed to ignore them. As a sign of this, Jacob continues to go through life as "Jacob," not by his new name of "Israel." He also continues living his life just as he did before the renaming. Renaming didn't change Jacob on the inside to the extent he needed, and Jacob could not become Israel until he underwent a serious attitude and life change. This is true for us as well—we cannot become renewed until we *act* as if we are renewed!

In Genesis 33 and 34 Jacob goes by his old name because he continues to live his old life. But, as time goes on, that begins to change. Jacob destroys foreign gods and commands his family and people to worship God (see Genesis 35). He even builds an altar. After all of this, God comes to Jacob again and re-blesses him. Jacob accepts the blessing this time and lets God do a work in him. At that point, Jacob ends and Israel begins.

Do you allow God to rename you, or do you struggle against Him and go by the same old name? How many times has God tried to bring a blessing upon you, but by your own actions you have shrugged those blessings off? Look back over the course of your life and try to recognize the good God has done for and in you. I guarantee you'll find many blessings you previously overlooked. But here's your chance—God is calling for an encore. He will give and give and give; when will you choose to take?

To think and pray about:

- What are you struggling with?

- What is making you doubt?

- Will you/have you let God rename you?

Whatever it is, remember how God has been there for you all the times in the past when the going has been rough.

"No matter the circumstance, God can turn your barriers into blessings."

#ABANDON

Chapter Nine

SPOILER ALERT

When I was a child, I loved to watch basketball. But the games were at night, and my father wanted to make sure I got to bed on time, so he made me record all the games to watch the next day. So of course, when I went to school the next day, I wouldn't want my friends to give me any details about the game or tell me who won. I didn't want to know how things would end; that would spoil the game for me.

But in real life, we're just the opposite. We *want* to know the ending. We want to know how everything will play out in our lives and where, exactly, we will end up. God, however, does life on a need-to-know basis. Think about Moses, for instance. God gave Moses a forty-year wilderness plan, but made him uncover each day one by one.

In Psalms 119:105, God tells us that He will be a lamp unto our feet. If you've ever walked with a lamp, you know that a lamp only illuminates a step or two at a time. All you can see is the path immediately in front of you, no further.

So when times are tough, and we're facing a mountain of trials, we can usually only see the immediacy of what's at hand. Even though God doesn't tell us in advance each and every step we're going to take on our life path, He *does* give us the ultimate spoiler alert—He tells us that at the end of the situation or circumstance you're facing, with faith in Christ Jesus, *we win.*

Unlike the basketball games of my youth, in this life it's good to know the ending. I'm glad to know that despite the work of the enemy, despite the adversities, I have hope. The fact that you are still fighting is proof that the struggle has not overtaken you.

> Even though God doesn't tell us in advance each and every step we're going to take on our life path, He *does* give us the ultimate spoiler alert—He tells us that at the end of the situation or circumstance you're facing, with faith in Christ Jesus, *we win.*
>
> #ABANDON

It's hard at times to remember that though, isn't it? Our minds work very hard not to change, and the enemy wants us to look at our situations as we see them and not as God does. His goal is to get us depressed by the things that we haven't accomplished yet or things that we need to work on but lack the resources to do. Focusing on the negative distracts us from realizing that tough seasons are temporary.

This is exactly what the enemy wants us to do! Don't let the enemy get what he wants.

The story of Jacob reminds us of our all-too-human tendency to do this. When Jacob dropped to the banks of the Jabbok River, he was focused on the fact that he had Laban at his rear and Esau up ahead, both out to get him. He had weighing heavy on him the stress and futility of the situation at hand. He could look no further than the immediacy of his situation and see any outcome that didn't leave him dead or suffering.

We all have times like this. The bills mount. The kids are acting up and failing at school. We're arguing non-stop with our spouse. The entire weight of the world is on our shoulders and there is no possible way we can do what needs to get done. Not without going crazy, anyway. Sometimes it even seems like the act of sleep gets in the way, and I wonder, "Why do I have to waste time resting? There's so much to do and so little time!"

Our minds work very hard not to change.
#ABANDON

Simply put, life isn't perfect. We have peaks and valleys, and in some seasons of life the valleys seem much deeper than the peaks seem high. Let's talk about how you can manage to see not only the light at the end of the tunnel, but also appreciate the place where you are right now.

A NEGATIVE MIND WILL NEVER PRODUCE A POSITIVE LIFE

There are plenty of things that can consume our time and keep our focus off of enjoying life. We must remember that we are the ones who make the decision whether or not to allow these things to affect us. We can't waste our tomorrows thinking about our yesterdays, and we can't spend all our hours dwelling on the negative things that haven't even happened yet, especially when there is so much beauty all around us.

I once read, *"Life is not measured by the number of breaths we take, but by the moments that take our breath away"* —VICKI CORONA, 1989.

What takes your breath away? If you aren't quite sure and you're looking for real-life, practical ways to start recognizing the glory that surrounds you, here is list of things to point you in the right direction:

1. **Appreciate God's Creations**: Every day we have the opportunity to see God's hand in all of creation—everything from humans to trees. It's a shame, then, that many people have become so accustomed to these beauties that they largely go unappreciated. Every day, take a moment to appreciate God's creations and identify what makes them so special.

2. **Value Family**: *"In every conceivable manner, the family is a link to our past, and a bridge to our future"* —ALEX HALEY.

3. **Build Relationships**: In many ways it is our relationships with people that give us the most happiness in life. *"There is great comfort and inspiration in the feeling of close human relationships and its bearing of mutual fortunes—a powerful force, to overcome the 'tough breaks,' which are certain to come to most of us from time to time"* —WALT DISNEY.

4. **Have Simple Pleasures**: My sister, Chris, says, *"Your morning has not started until you pray and have a nice hot cup of tea."* That's her simple pleasure; take the time to enjoy these ordinary events and life will become more enjoyable.

5. **Listen and Learn**: Life can be very rewarding, especially when we grasp the concept that listening + learning = happiness.

6. **Laugh, Laugh, Laugh**: Did you know that laughter reduces stress hormones, wards off depression, cleanses the lungs, relaxes the muscles, enhances the immune system, and reduces pain and blood pressure? Never become too busy for laughter; the more you laugh the better you feel. *"The most wasted of all days is one without laughter"* —E.E. CUMMINGS.

7. **Celebrate Your Successes**: Oftentimes in life we can't enjoy our major victories because we're thinking about the minor failures we encountered on the way. Take a moment to celebrate your successes. When you accomplish these victories, whether large or small, reward yourself with some gesture of accomplishment.

8. **Remember that your value isn't based on your valuables.** Your value is based on the simple fact of your creation and being.

9. Some final advice:

    In happy moments, praise God.
    In difficult moments, seek God.
    In quiet moments, worship God.
    In painful moments, trust God.
    In every moment, thank God.
    —AUTHOR UNKNOWN

I WON'T GO BACK

The Australian coat of arms has two animals on it—the kangaroo and the emu. These animals are very significant because they have a difficult time with moving backward. This may seem like a negative attribute to some, but the people of Australia knew better. They knew that the inability to move backward is actually a *strength*, and this is why both animals earned a spot on the Australian shield. They represent a people moving forward, steadfastly refusing to go backward.

They knew that the inability to move
backward is actually a *strength*.

#ABANDON

We can learn a lot from these two animals. Once we put the love and word of faith of God into our lives, we must move forward in that, never looking back to our old lives and ways. We must live our lives forward, looking toward the possibilities of what could be instead of wasting so much time re-living the past and what could have been. And more than anything, we must do so with gratitude and joy.

Do you see the glass as half empty or half full? Jacob, through the work of God in him, successfully changed from a viewpoint of half empty to an attitude of half full. He moved forward faithfully, carrying joy with him.

We see in the story of Jacob that he faced many, many sorrows. As in all of our lives, Jacob had highs and lows, and he took them all in stride. Even though Jacob's life did not ever become one of ease, it became changed, just as Jacob himself became changed. Jacob was able to accept his blessing without attempting to make deals, fix things himself, or deceive his way out of tough or unwanted seasons of life. Instead, he finally learned to abandon his life to God.

This is a good lesson to carry with us when times get tough: God is always present and doing His handiwork. His Word doesn't say He will remove you from the situation. It says He will be with you in the midst of the situation. Even when it seems nothing is going right, God is faithful and He will prove His faithfulness through His protection and provision. He has placed us here on earth to *live*, so stop just merely existing. Put your trust in Him and take the time today to enjoy today!

The Bible gives us hope and the knowledge that we, as God's children, can wake up each day to blessings, large and small. When we take notice of that and grab hold of the powerful truth that God stands in our yesterday, today, and tomorrow, we will see that with the help of God failure is not an option. The ending of our life's story reads—*we win*.

To consider:

- What simple pleasure can you add to your everyday life?

- Take some time to notice the world around you. What takes your breath away?

- Do you feel like you're living life or waiting for "real" life to begin?

- No more waiting! How can you get started living your life today?

"*Focusing on the negative distracts us from realizing that tough seasons are temporary.*"

#ABANDON

ABOUT TIM TIMBERLAKE

Tim Timberlake is the lead pastor of Christian Faith Center in Creedmoor, North Carolina. He is a gifted communicator and teacher and has the ability to minister to people of all cultures and generations through his in-depth Bible teaching, sense of humor, and leading of the Holy Spirit.

God has given him a vision and a heart for helping people meet Jesus, and each week he teaches the Word in a format for people to apply it in their daily lives.

Tim is a graduate of the Pistis School of Ministry in Detroit, Michigan. He is an avid sports fan and a popular thought leader.